IMMIGRANT FURNITURE WORKERS IN LONDON 1881-1939

and the Jewish contribution to the Furniture Trade

William I. Massil

THE JEWISH MUSEUM
IN ASSOCIATION WITH THE GEFFRYE MUSEUM

Published in 1997 by The Jewish Museum, London
in association with The Geffrye Museum, London E2
ISBN 1 871447 04 6
Copyright © William I. Massil and The Jewish Museum 1997

The Jewish Museum, Finchley
80 East End Road
London N3 2SY

The Jewish Museum, Camden Town
Raymond Burton House
129-131 Albert Street
London NW1 7NB

Dedicated to the memory of my father
Hyman Massil (1881-1946),
woodturner and master of his trade,
whose example has been an inspiration to me.

Front illustration: Horse and cart delivering furniture made by Lebus, London, 1902.
Courtesy of the Lebus Archives, Victoria and Albert Museum.
Back illustration: Delivering Lebus furniture, c.1908.
Courtesy of the Lebus Archives, Victoria and Albert Museum.

CONTENTS

LIST OF ILLUSTRATIONS

ACKNOWLEDGMENTS

This history of the immigrant furniture-workers was born at a dinner table in North London some years ago. My host was Dr Harold Rose, a well-known chemical engineer, and one of the other guests was Sidney Lawrence, a pharmaceutical chemist. Both of their fathers had been cabinet makers in East London in the early 1900's. Lawrence's father had graduated to the ranks of the veneer merchants, but Barnett Rosenberg remained a cabinet maker all his life, moving from job to job, at one time having a managerial position at S. Hille & Co.

I found myself able to tell both Harold and Sidney exactly where their fathers had worked and traded, because of my intimate knowledge of the geography and structure of the East End furniture trade. Harold was intrigued by my close knowledge of the trade and insisted that I write up the whole story. I reluctantly agreed and over a number of years, by dint of much delving into people's memories, the following account of the development of the trade has emerged. It now seems clear to me that this is in fact possibly the last opportunity for such a detailed account of this subject to be produced, based on personal interviews and experience.

I have to thank the many people who have co-operated by providing me with interviews. They are mainly the sons and daughters of the original immigrants, many of whom I would have had the privilege of working with, as my father's firm was engaged in woodturning, almost exclusively for the furniture makers of the time. Among those who have given copious assistance are Gerald Abrahams, Mrs Arenson and family, the late Frank Austin, Lionel and Roy Bianco, Gerald Burke, members of the Burkle family, Oliver Lebus, Jack Moss (of FTAT), Ewart Myer, Mr Rust of HK Furniture, members of the Schreiber family, Mick Serlin, members of the Serota family, Jack Sklan, Jack and Lily Summers (Sadow) and Jeffrey Wiseman. I have endeavoured to record as accurately as possible dates and places of work, but it is inevitable that some facts and incidents have tended to become blurred after a long passage of time.

I would like to express my gratitude to the members of the Hille family who were instrumental in arranging for Mrs Ray Hille to be "taped" by me when she was in poor health at the age of 85, three months before her death, and also for their permission to use a number of photographs from their archive.

I am greatly indebted to Rickie Burman, the Director of the Jewish Museum, London, and to her staff, and to David Dewing, the Director of the Geffrye Museum, London and to his staff. I should like to thank Professor William Fishman and Dr David Feldman for their advice and guidance, and Dr A. Joseph and Dr M. Jolles for their assistance.

I should also mention my daughter Janet Newman and her husband David - himself a son and grandson of timber trade immigrants - without whose help this work would have been quite impossible. My son, Stephen, a librarian and active member of the Executive of the Jewish Historical Society of England, has also been most helpful in many ways. I should also like to express my appreciation of my wife Eileen, who has been long-suffering in listening to my innumerable repetitions of incidents and eccentricities I have come across in researching this project.

I am grateful for the help given to me by Sidney Frosh who, as sales director of S. Greenman Ltd was a fund of information on immigrant furniture firms in the provinces.

Another fruitful source of information has been the back issues of *The Cabinet Maker*, the leading furniture trade journal, which, by coincidence, was founded in July 1880 - just before the years of the greatest influx of furniture-making immigrants - and has recently celebrated its 5,000th issue at the time of writing.

I should like to thank all the individuals and organisations who have provided illustrations and granted permission for them to be reproduced in the book: *The Cabinet Maker*, Roy Bianco, Ronald Chapman, The Geffrye Museum, Hille International Ltd, The Jewish Museum, London, James Latham Ltd, Oliver Lebus, London Metropolitan Archive, London Borough of Hackney Archives Department, Vestry House Museum, London, The Victoria and Albert Museum and Jeffrey Wiseman.

I am also grateful to the British Library, *The Cabinet Maker* and *The Jewish Chronicle* for their cooperation in permitting the obituaries of Archy Arenson and Harris Lebus to be reproduced in the book, and to publishers John Baker and A & E Black Ltd for their assistance in allowing information provided in Kenneth Hudson's book *Where We Used to Work* to be used (Appendix 2).

I have of course found it impossible to include all the immigrants and the firms which they set up, and to all those whom I should have mentioned, or persevered in locating or included in greater detail, I offer my unreserved apologies. I hope, however, that they will find something of interest and relevance to the history of their families' connection with the trade.

The Jewish Museum, together with the Geffrye Museum, acknowledges with thanks the following individuals and organisations whose financial support has made possible the publication of this book.

**The Archy Arenson Charitable Trust
Sir Geoffrey Leigh**

Mr John Agram
Mr Alan Cohen
Mr Edmund Cohen
Mr Leonard Fertleman
Heron International
Mr William Massil
Mrs Schreiber
Mr Philip Steinberg
Universal Fittings

FUNDED BY

LONDON
BOROUGHS
GRANTS
COMMITTEE

CHAPTER 1

The Background

The story I have to tell concerns the many hundreds of workers in the furniture trade who came mainly from Russia, Poland and Romania, and settled in London at the end of the 19th century and at the beginning of the 20th century. I am confining my account to the predominantly Jewish immigrants who came to Britain in this period.[1] They were mainly skilled cabinet makers, who produced all kinds of domestic furniture, or carpenters, with a sprinkling of other associated trades, such as woodturners, carvers, marquetry workers and so on, who had been practising these skills in their home countries before they left. I shall refer here, however, generally to "furniture workers" rather than "cabinet makers" as the furniture industry contained various types of skilled craftsmen.

The Jewish furniture workers arrived here with little or no money or goods, no language except Yiddish or the language of their native country. Some were already married and with families, but the majority were young and unattached. The main objective that they had in common was to establish themselves in productive work and make new homes in what they hoped would be a less hostile environment than that from which they had fled. Many of my older readers will remember incidents regarding cabinet makers of that period; they and their parents may have had recourse to a "little man in the East End", who would have produced for them some very fine furniture at ridiculously cheap prices.

I feel sure that very few of these immigrants had any idea of building large businesses or financial empires. However, as the story unfolds, I hope to show how a number of these immigrants laid the foundations of very substantial enterprises in a relatively short period of time. I can name a few of the firms which became household names by the time of the Second World War and then into the 1950s. These include companies such as Beautility, J. Summers and Sons, B. & I. Nathan, Austinsuite, Stonehill, Lazarus, Bluestone & Elvin, Hille & Co, H. & L. Epstein, B. Cohen & Sons, Palatial Furniture and the companies of the Serlin family and many others. Some of the smaller firms, such as Gabe & Pass, Serota, Herman & Philips, were producing furniture of the highest quality and became quite renowned. They would supply retail shops of the calibre of Maples and Waring & Gillow and extended their market into Scotland to firms such as Wylie & Lochhead.

During the Second World War every medium and large-scale factory devoted their efforts to producing ammunition boxes, landing craft, even aircraft components and repairing aircraft. The smaller firms, struggling with chronic shortages of any form of raw materials, were also eventually drafted into the production of officially sanctioned Utility furniture.

As I write today, however, there are very few of these firms remaining, most of the descendants having joined the ranks of the professions, commerce or finance.

My own connection in the trade goes back to the late 1920s in the Shoreditch area which was the hub of the industry at that time, taking in Curtain Road, Old Street, Great Eastern Street, Hackney Road and Bethnal Green, and stretching into Hackney, Stoke Newington, Clapton and Stepney. My firm also followed the pattern of many of these firms who later moved out into modern factories in the suburbs and beyond.

Note

1   Immigrant communities have contributed to the furniture trade in England from the mid 17th century onwards, when Dutch, Huguenot and other French craftsmen started to arrive. The Welsh-Huguenot firm of H. Vaughan Ltd. still occupies premises in the East End after more than three hundred years in the trade and their history has been published (Vaughan, 1984).

CHAPTER 2

The London Furniture Trade
in the Early Nineteenth Century

Before discussing the many immigrant furniture workers after 1881, it is important to examine the make-up of the existing English trade, its conditions of work and its marketing arrangements when they arrived.

In the early part of the 19th century, the London furniture-manufacturing trade consisted of mainly small workshops, and was divided between London's West End - the "honourable" side - and the East End - the "dishonourable" side. Up to about 1850 the West End makers supplied the prestigious retailers in Tottenham Court Road, after which the East End started to take over as suppliers. The general conception has been that the West End produced only "good" quality and the East End "cheap" quality, but there were many deviations from these norms. The West End - around Tottenham Court Road and the back streets - had workshops where "shoddy" work was produced, while the East End had shops where superb work was made, and this pattern was maintained by the Jewish immigrants who settled almost exclusively in the East End. Many of them were skilled craftsmen and were able to interpret and embellish the prevailing English reproduction styles. These fine craftsmen were later to establish highly respected companies such as Gabe & Pass, Morris Ruben, Serota & Cohen and a whole host of others.

The working conditions in the 19th century were mainly very bad and sometimes appalling. "Sweat shops" were the order of the day and these are described very well by Charles Booth in his *Life and*

Labour of the People in London (1888), and by Henry Mayhew in *London Labour and the London Poor* (1851). In 1850 Mayhew also published 82 letters in *The Morning Chronicle*, of which nine dealt with wood workers and gave a remarkable insight into the conditions and economic stringency surrounding furniture workers and even the "small masters" in the furniture trade. One of the worst offenders in this context seems to have been the firm of Maples, pre-eminent in the West End retail trade, who purchased their wares from both West End and East End cabinet makers. They were largely responsible for the "sweat shop" conditions which obtained, as they were in a powerful position to squeeze the makers into fierce competition with each other because of their strong market-position over this period.

In the East End, the owners of small firms with one to five employees and an owner working on the bench were called "garret masters" and very often worked above or behind where they lived. They worked on a cash basis, from week to week, selling their products initially to well-established wholesalers in and around Curtain Road in Shoreditch.

These wholesalers were usually not Jewish. They produced nothing, but had the capital, space and linguistic and business skills to purchase finished goods from the small makers and then to sell them on to retailers in the West End such as Maples, Waring & Gillow, Oetzman, Bartholomew & Fletcher, Shoolbred, Woolfe and Hollander and also to various provincial retailers.

There was also a large export trade to countries of the British Empire, Argentina and the U.S.A. In the 18th and 19th centuries Britain was the largest exporter of furniture in Europe. In 1830, the total value of furniture work exported was £55,000, but by 1850 the figure had almost doubled to £100,000 and by 1888 it had reached no less than £750,000 of which almost a third went to Australia, and the rest to South Africa, Argentina and the U.S.A. (Kirkham 1987).

During the second half of the 19th century there was sporadic trade union organization in the furniture trade. However, this was not very effective, partly as many of the workers were always aiming to become their own masters, even though in this position they were often unable to earn as much as their workers initially, unless they had a number of their own children working for them. If their businesses failed, they would go back to the bench and try again later.

As far as the existing English trade was concerned, it was also a time of some change. Thus it is one of the ironies of this story that, at the precise time when these immigrant furniture-makers were arriving and settling in the East End, C. R. Ashbee was moving with his native English furniture craftsmen from the same area of London to set up an idyllic community of craftspeople in the Cotswolds. He was following the ruralist example of the Barnsley brothers and Ernest Gimson who had pioneered the "Arts and Crafts" movement in furniture-making in small workshops outside the cities. As far as I can ascertain there was no contact between these groups.

It is of further interest to note that, although many of the better craftsmen among the immigrants made every style of English period furniture from Elizabethan Tudor through Jacobean, William and Mary, Queen Anne and the Georgian periods, and ultimately the Regency style, I have not come across any examples of them making any furniture in the Arts and Crafts or other styles actually being designed at that time. This is probably due to market-demand from retailers and wholesalers, whereas demand for Arts and Craft style seems to have been limited to smaller, if more élite, outlets such as Liberty's and Heal's.

Thus, to sum up the situation in the trade when the furniture-makers started arriving in force, there were a large number of small woodworking firms in the West End and in the East End. The West End makers would supply the retailers in Tottenham Court Road, while the East End makers would supply the wholesalers in Curtain Road and also the West End retailers to some extent.

In most cases, with shortage of capital and facilities, the manufacturing firms were very small and working on a shoestring, where they barely made a living and their workers were on a low level of earnings and worked under very bad conditions.

By the end of the 19th century, however, several larger firms existed which had been set up by a smaller number of earlier immigrants. The most striking of these is the firm established by Louis Lebus, who in fact seems to have been the earliest recorded Jewish immigrant furniture worker. It is noted in a history of the firm written by a descendant, Louis S.Lebus, that he arrived in Hull from Breslau in the 1840s. By 1881 his firm was already relatively substantial, working out of a number of small workshops, and its continuing dramatic development by the second generation is treated at some length in later chapters. Another large company, I. Herrmann, of uncertain immigrant origin, had a similarly large plant at Dod Street, Limehouse. In these larger firms, established by earlier immigrants, Yiddish was generally spoken by management and supervisory staffs, so that they were able to communicate with the later immigrants from 1881 onwards in their own language.

CHAPTER 3

Earlier Immigrant Furniture Workers

There had been a small nucleus of Jewish people living in the City of London before Cromwell allowed the re-admission of the Jews to England in 1656. However there then began a small but steady stream of Jewish immigrants, mainly Sephardi at first, and later Ashkenazi, who set up their own synagogues. There were also groups from Germany, Russia, Poland and Romania even before the period of mass migration which took place in the years between 1881 and 1914.

I have already mentioned the Lebus family who were the most famous of the earlier immigrant furniture workers and whose firm grew to an enormous size by furniture industry standards. By 1857 Louis Lebus had established a workshop in Whitechapel Eighteen years later, he had moved to larger premises in Wellclose Square in Stepney. After his death in 1879 his 27-year old son Harris, took over the business, and in 1885 moved the firm to still larger, multi-storey premises in Tabernacle Street near to the centre of the trade in Curtain Road, Shoreditch.

In 1894 there was a disastrous fire at the factory, and, by 1899 after rebuilding, Lebus was employing no less than 1,000 operative (most of whom were immigrants) and 45 managerial staff. They were by far the largest furniture firm in the country and were producing mainly quite high quality bedroom suites and some dining sets and had invested in a large amount of modern machinery Further expansion was planned, and in 1900 Lebus decided to move out to Tottenham into what was then countryside, where a site of thirteen and a half acres was purchased. This was later increased t no less than 40 acres. By 1903-4 a factory had been built and most of the workers commuted by tram from the East End. The workers, however, found the travelling and loss of time unsatisfactory so Lebus and others arranged the building of large numbers of houses in the South Tottenham area. Thus a Jewish community was born in Tottenham, and Baum and Glick (1982) record that, as there was no synagogue in the area, a room was set aside in the factory as a temporary place of worship.

At the turn of the century, there were two other fairly large Jewish-owned firms in the Tottenham area. One was Gestetner's, a firm making copying equipment, which was founded by David Gestetner, an immigrant from Germany, in Sun Street, Finsbury, and subsequently moved to Tottenham in 1904. The other Jewish firm established in the area was Flatau's, shoe and slipper manufacturers.

The next immigrant furniture manufacturer in degree of importance was Barnett Cohen, who set up as a cabinet maker, coincidentally also in Sun Street, Finsbury in 1848. His firm was to become famous as B. Cohen & Sons Ltd. After several moves, a large factory was established at 7/19 Curtain Road, making high class furniture of all kinds until the Second World War.

Another early imigrant was Abraham Myer (1796-1872), who came from the Rhineland in Germany to Cheltenham in about 1815 and had no immediate connection with the furniture trade. In his book *Myer's First Century 1876-1976* Ewart Myer notes that his great-grandfather Abraham eventually settled in Hereford, setting up first as a pawnbroker, and later expanding to the dignity of "jeweller, silversmith, watchmaker and fashionable clothing establishment." His son, Horatio (1850-1916) first went into the wool trade locally, and eventually by 1876 had purchased a firm in Vauxhall producing iron bedsteads; this firm was to become the well known and still flourishing firm of Horatio Myer & Co Ltd, whose headquarters are now in Huntingdon. For many years their main product has been divans of various sorts with the popular slogan: "Myers for comfortable beds". I have no knowledge of any Jewish employees in this firm in recent times other than a Mr Levy who was on their sales staff for many years, but it may be of interest to note that there is a tombstone in a very prominent position at the Willesden Jewish Cemetery to Horatio Myer who died in Hereford in 1916.

Morris Ruben was another early immigrant, born in Vilna, Lithuania, in 1864, and brought to London by his parents at three years of age. After education at the Jews' Free School (then in the East End) he was apprenticed to his father Jacob. By 1887 he was self-employed with six staff, making the finest quality furniture, and by 1900 there were 35 employees, increasing to 200 by 1914. Unfortunately the firm closed upon the death of the founder in 1926, but when I joined the furniture trade in 1928, the name of Morris Ruben was mentioned in awe as a maker of the highest quality furniture.

CHAPTER 4

Immigrant Furniture Workers after 1881

My research suggests that by far the majority of the immigrant furniture workers in the East End after 1881 were Jews. By 1850, Vivian Lipman tells us in *The Social History of the Jews 1850-1950* there were 18,000 Jews in London, and 35,000 in the whole of Great Britain. By 1881, however, this total had risen to about 65,000 in Great Britain, and, by 1914, the number was estimated to be between 250,000 and 300,000. This enormous increase in the Jewish population in Britain from 1881 onwards is attributed to the oppressive conditions of life under the Tsarist regime in Russia, the pogroms that occurred after the murder of Alexander II in Russia, and a concerted drive to conscript young Jewish boys into the Russian army for periods of up to 25 years.

Lipman's analysis of the occupations of British Jews gives 1% to 2% working in the furniture trade, whilst by 1901 this share had increased to between 5% to 10%, and by 1950, he reported that there were 8,000 to 10,000 Jews in the furniture trade in East London alone. Those immigrants who were woodworkers were either cabinet makers, joiners, carpenters, wheelwrights or coopers, or skilled in the specialist ancillary trades such as carving, turning and veneering.[1] It should be remembered that at that time practically all furniture was made by hand with simple tools, with the exception of very few firms such as Lebus and Herrmann.

The many thousands of immigrants coming to Britain, either to settle or migrate onwards to North or South America or to South Africa, found the communal organizations unprepared to handle the influx. However, at some time between 1882 and 1885, a private individual named Simcha Becker, himself a recent immigrant and baker, organised shelter and food in limited quantities in his own home and in the adjoining bakery. The leaders of the Anglo-Jewish community learnt about this initiative and, in April 1885, Lionel Alexander and Frederic Mocatta of the Jewish Board of Guardians paid a surprise visit to the house and declared the facilities unhealthy. This led to its closure by the intercession of the Jewish Board of Guardians, but positive help for the immigrants came from three wealthy supporters - Hermann Landau, a Polish immigrant of 1864, Sir Samuel Montagu, the M.P. for Whitechapel, and Ellis Franklin (who himself later became an M.P.). They jointly financed a more satisfactory building and the "Poor Jews' Temporary Shelter" opened in Leman Street, Aldgate in October 1885. This served as a centre for Jewish immigrants and trans-migrants, providing food and lodgings to newcomers. While some immigrants had family members who had already settled in London, others arrived completely alone with few possessions, no money and speaking only Yiddish and/or Russian, Polish or Rumanian.

In studying the records at the Jews' Temporary Shelter from 1897 onwards, one can see that a typical immigrants' ship arrived from Hamburg carrying several hundred Jews from Lithuania, who were then housed at the Shelter for two or three days, before being shipped on to South Africa. Each person was entered into the record book and all his details such as marital status, children, town or village of origin, trade etc, were noted. It appears that this Shelter alone was responsible for processing up to 4,000 immigrants each year between 1885 and 1914.

All individuals and families were housed and fed for a maximum of 14 days and then had to make their own way - either to relatives or to lodgings and a job. In examining the records of trades recorded at the Shelter, it is interesting to note that the description "cabinet maker" very rarely appears, but that "carpenter" appears regularly. However, it should be noted that the same Yiddish word *stoller* covers both meanings.

Note

1   Women were not generally employed in the furniture trades, except in polishing and upholstery, generally regarded as the most unpleasant jobs in the industry, and in fact, Jewish women did not take up these activities to any great extent.

CHAPTER 5

The East London Furniture Trade
in the 1880's and 1890's

At the time of the great influx of Jewish immigrants to Britain in the 1880's and 1890's, the structure of the furniture trade in East London consisted of four elements:

(1) A number of non-manufacturing wholesalers situated in and around Curtain Road, Great Eastern Street and the City (Finsbury), mainly owned by gentiles,

(2) Two or three relatively large firms which were mainly mechanised (such as Harris Lebus and H. Herrmann) employing between 500 and 1,000 people,

(3) A few medium-sized firms employing 50 to 100 people

and:

(4) A very large number of small workshops with working proprietors and up to six employees based mainly in the Bethnal Green area.

The new Jewish immigrants - commonly called "greeners" in the Jewish community - had to find their employment at Lebus's or at one of the other medium-sized firms where Yiddish was spoken.

The following examples, taken from back issues of *The Cabinet Maker* from 1880 onwards, provide a cross-section of typical firms, most of which have now ceased to exist.

- Clozenberg & Sons, Curtain Road, Shoreditch, and Charlotte Street (off Old Street), established in 1850. By 1891 their factory covered 11,390 sq.ft. and employed 120 workers.

- N. Glickstein of Great Eastern Street, Shoreditch, in 1891 employing 100 workers.

- Saul Moss & Sons of Curtain Road and Liverpool (itself a smaller centre of Jewish immigration), established in 1843.

- H. L. Benjamin, established in Scrutton Street ,off Great Eastern Street in 1889, moving to larger premises in 1898.

- B. Cohen & Sons, established in 1848, quite a large firm in Curtain Road by this time.

- Harris Lebus who in 1899 had a full page advertisement in *The Cabinet Maker* claiming to be "the largest cabinet manufacturer in the United Kingdom."

- H. Herrmann of Dod Street, E.14, who claimed in the same issue in 1899 to be "the largest cabinet manufacturer in Europe", but who faded out later as manufacturers.

- I. Griew & Co must have been well established. *The Cabinet Maker* of March 1904 records that Isaac Griew and Paul Joseph had dissolved their partnership continuing as I. Griew & Co with premises at 53-55 Hoxton Square, 1-2 Victoria Buildings and 8-14 Coronet Street in Hoxton.

- Rosenstreich & Co of 154-160 City Road and Peerless Street, Hoxton, was established in 1854 but went into bankruptcy in 1905.

- Glickstein & Co Ltd was formed in 1905 with registered capital of £1,000 to acquire the existing business of S. Glickstein and I. Glickstein to trade as Glickstein & Co, cabinet-makers and timber-merchants. This firm was to become one of the largest British importers of hardwood and plywood under the name of S. Glicksten (sic) with the later generations of the founding family becoming well known as directors of Millwall Football Club.

- C. Weinberg of Motley Street, Curtain Road, producers of good quality Chippendale and "Louis" cabinets.

- J. Schuman & Co Ltd of 1 Rufus Street, near Old Street specialised in bookcases. I believe that this firm had a family connection with I.Griew & Co.

The high level of immigration caused some problems with the indigenous population, culminating in the restrictive Aliens' Act of 1905. It appears that the furniture trade, and no doubt other trades, were passing through a difficult time during the 1880s and 1890s, and as usual blame had been apportioned to "infiltration" by 'aliens'. However, a different view was taken by liberals like Charles Booth, who dealt with the issue of competition from Jews and from other foreign immigrants in his *Life and Labour of the People in London* (1888-93), in a section dealing with East London trades, as follows:

"As distinct causes these two elements seem to be imaginary rather than real, but constant reference is made to them ... and it has become indeed a habit with many to look to them for the solutions of many of the disturbing phenomena of the East London trades."

Booth then went on to say:

"It seems, however, that neither of them can rightly be regarded as original sources of disturbance. For the majority of the Jews and foreigners enter into the trade in precisely the same way that Englishmen do. In this group of trades, the former cannot be said to set in motion a fresh chain of causes that are powerful either for harm or for good, but must be regarded as being subject to the same wider and more fundamental influences that are already at work and which tend to affect all alike, whatever their creed or race may be."

Booth estimated in fact that in 1888 there were only about 700 Jewish workers in the East London furniture trade. This assessment may not be inconsistent with Lipman's figures quoted earlier but is possibly an under-estimate. Of this group, he found 76 who were apprentices placed by the Board of Guardians of British Jews between 1884 and 1888, quite a high proportion, considering that apprenticeship took five years at low wages. The assistance provided by the Board at that time was considered exemplary, as is evident from a letter in *The Cabinet Maker* of December 1885 from Mr A.P. Chatterton, a teacher of cabinet-making and of apprentices, regarding a meeting of teachers:

"I made a suggestion that a fund should be formed upon the lines of that organised by the Jewish Board of Guardians for our own gentile lads."

This might also indicate that great importance was attached to the acquisition of high quality skills by the immigrants for their children. However, my experience is that not all immigrant furniture workers went through the rigours of formal apprenticeship but that many similarly learnt informally from the existing workforce.

CHAPTER 6

Early Furniture Trade Unions

There had been sporadic attempts to form trade unions in the London furniture trade in the eighteenth century, and in the 1760's the "honourable" West End furniture trades had set up permanent "trade societies". However, organising the furniture workers in the East End proved to be more difficult. Thus, in the Geffrye Museum's book, *Furnishing the World: The East London Furniture Trade 1830-1980* (Kirkham 1987), it was stated:

> "Trade Union organisation in this skilled section of the trade was far from easy or complete but the task was much more difficult in the East End. There, in the 19th century, subcontracting, long hours, low wages, the ease of transfer from worker to independent master or small employer, small isolated workshops, the complete collapse of the apprenticeship system, an acute division of labour and the dual threat of youth, labour and unemployment militated against any, let alone effective, trade unionism."

After a number of attempts to form unions linked with the Chartist movement, the Alliance Cabinet Makers Association (ACMA) was formed in 1865. Meetings were held in Alliance Hall in Old Street Road instead of in public houses, as was the practice at that time, in order to present a more "respectable" image.

In 1893 a number of small societies, including the Hebrew Cabinet Makers' Society, joined the Alliance, whose total membership increased in that year by 423 of whom about 200 were from the Hebrew Society. Reid mentions in *The Furniture Makers* that the

Alliance rules were translated into "Hebrew" at a cost of 5 guineas - he probably meant Yiddish in fact.

However this change was not universally well received:

> "Not all Jewish workers felt comfortable in the new association, despite the fact that some of the ACMA branches were now heavily dominated by Jewish workers. Some also objected to the Union's campaign against piece work and broke away to form the independent Hebrew Society in 1895." (from *Furnishing the World op cit*)

By 1902, however, the Alliance was merged with other unions to form NAFTA, the National Amalgamated Furnishing Trades Association. It was NAFTA which was responsible for organising the workers in the emerging factories in growing numbers in East London, and the person largely responsible for this was Sidney Fineman, himself a cabinet maker, and the son of an immigrant cabinet maker.

One of the problems of organising the Jewish East End workers was that many of them were hoping to become employers themselves rather than seeing themselves as long-term employees. Yet it should be noted that many remained at the bench throughout their working lives.

CHAPTER 7

Where did they work ?

Among the first requirements of the immigrants were a job and a home. It appears that the vast majority found work in the very large firms we have already noted. The remainder went to the smaller workshops, such as Isaac Griew and several others where Yiddish was the *lingua franca*. It was in fact common practice for the larger firms to send representatives down to the docks to await the arrival of the boats carrying the immigrants and to offer them employment as they disembarked. I understand that Lebus was said to have advertised for workers in the Jewish communities in Poland and Russia.

However, it is worth noting that many firms, once established, provided employment for non-Jews, and in my own case, when I joined my father in the 1920's, his workforce of six was entirely non-Jewish. There were also a few cases where firms such as S. Goldstein of Hoxton Street, Poplar Manufacturing Co, Rosen & Jones and Anjo Cabinet Works (an alliance between a Pole, Charlie Angelus, and a Mr Jones) came to be owned jointly by immigrant craftsmen and local gentiles who provided complementary commercial skills. The pre-eminent example of this cooperation was the august firm of Beresford & Hicks which is discussed at greater length in a later chapter.

The smaller firms often allowed the men to sleep in the workshops until they obtained lodgings or lived with relatives already established here. I believe that my own father, Hyman, a woodturner who arrived here about 1905, was employed by Franklin & Goldberg in Hackney Road, and he slept under his bench in his early days here. It must be remembered that most of the men were young, adventurous and, most likely, single. It seems that as soon as they had steady jobs, they were often introduced to young women, also working, most likely in the clothing trades. There was big business here for the traditional *shadchan* or matchmaker !

Within a relatively short space of time - one to five years - the more adventurous or enterprising were setting up in business, no doubt making the same sort of furniture as their erstwhile employers, but cutting the prices because of their limited overheads in the early stages of their business ventures.

They needed very little capital, as little or no machinery was used on their own premises, and as much of the rough machining of the timber was done in a number of jobbing "trade mills" in the East End. They were involved in long hours of very arduous manual labour.

In this context I am including here a list of immigrant furniture workers (Appendix 1) showing their dates of birth, where they came from, dates of arrival in London, and the dates when they first set up in business. Most of the information I obtained from their sons and daughters and in some cases the dates or other details are incomplete or uncertain.

Also included is a list of workshops in East London in the early 1920's (Appendix 2), reproduced from *Where We Used to Work* by Kenneth Hudson. In brackets he lists the number of "Jewish" firms in each street, using the names of the firms as a basis for their classification. It is noteworthy that some East End streets seem to have contained only workshops owned by Jews and I calculate approximately two-thirds of the workshops to have been of Jewish ownership. This list is a guide to the prodigious enterprise and intense involvement shown by new immigrants with no English language and little or no capital, who set up independently in business often within five to ten years of their arrival.

The establishment of the Jewish furniture workers within the East End was symbolised in the early 1920's by the founding of the United Workmen's and Wlodowa Synagogue at 21 Hare Street, off Brick Lane. This synagogue was formed by a group of immigrant craftsmen and named after a small town in Poland from which a number of them came. Harry Blacker, the son of a founder member, described the realization of this project as follows:

> "After a hard day's work, my father would come home, eat his dinner and then go off to the site, where he and many other craftsmen worked until midnight making seats, cupboards, doors, an ark and *bimah* for the proposed synagogue. In time, when this task was completed, a Hebrew class was opened in the rooms above." (Blacker 1974)

CHAPTER 8

Some Outstanding Firms of Immigrant Origin

As already mentioned, many firms were started by the immigrants and often were developed by members of the following generations of their families. In most cases there is no trace of family connections today in the few of these firms that still continue to exist. In this chapter, however, I have felt it worthwhile to sketch details of a number of these firms, in chronological order of the arrival of their respective founders.

The firms listed must necessarily form a personal selection from the many which no doubt would merit equal attention, but, in various ways, they seem to me to represent firms outstanding by virtue either of the size attained, or by the quality or type of work they produced, or by the sheer enterprise of the individuals concerned.

Harris Lebus (Immigration 1840)
Something of the early history of this firm has already been mentioned. It became outstanding in size and in innovation of production methods. Harris Lebus, the son of the founder who had arrived in 1840, merits special mention as he was largely responsible for the tremendous development of the firm from its very small size when he took over in 1879 up to his untimely death in 1907 at the age of 55, and I therefore intend to discuss his enormous personal contribution to the development of the British trade in my concluding chapter.

The large size of the company by 1912 can be seen from one of the photographs included here, which shows the large number of young women then employed in part of Lebus's polishing shop. It is worth noting that this operation was seen as one of the most unpleasant jobs in the industry, and it was common practice in the trade at this time to employ women only for polishing and upholstery work.

The growth of the firm was, however, astonishing, as by the time of the Second World War they were employing some 7,000 to 8,000 workers. After the war the site of some 40 acres was sold to the London County Council for housing and the firm seems to have declined and disintegrated. Although the Harris Lebus name is still in use at the time of writing, there is no longer any family connection.

B. Cohen & Sons (Immigration c. 1840)

Another outstanding firm was founded by an earlier immigrant, Barnett Cohen, who was born in 1815 and arrived in England, probably in the 1840's. However, he is known to have set up in business in 1848 in Sun Street in Finsbury in the City of London In 1867 his youngest son, Abraham, joined him at the age of 16, obtaining all-round experience in the trade. In 1871 a move was made to small premises at 148 Curtain Road, Shoreditch, and four years later No. 11 Curtain Road was acquired, the first section of the site which was to become a very large factory. By 1880 another son, Michael, had joined the business which became known as B Cohen & Sons. Although machinery was being introduced and furniture was produced in relatively large quantities, all production was nonetheless of a particularly high quality.

In the First World War, the firm went over to a whole range of war work including aeroplane propellers. In the Second World War they were engaged in the production of very large quantities of furniture for the whole range of the armed services. The factory was bombed, but continued making "utility" furniture and the firm finally left Curtain Road in 1952. Richard Cohen, however, continued in a small way of business, manufacturing one-off "specials" and joinery outside the East End on the Cambridge Arterial Road, and indeed produced an informative booklet in 1958 celebrating the centenary of the company's establishment. The firm ceased production in 1968.

Beresford & Hicks (Immigration 1870)
Julius B. Wiszniewski was a gentile piano maker in Danzig (now Gdansk) in Poland. He came to London in the 1870's and met Richard Hicks who married Wiszniewski's twin sister in 1875. At some stage he took the name Julius Beresford and together they formed Beresford & Hicks in 1891 with a factory in Hemsworth Street, Hoxton, and a showroom in Curtain Road, Shoreditch. By 1918 they were known as "manufacturing upholsterers and framemakers" with a large showroom at 135 to 139 Curtain Road adorned with its own telegraphic address. They later produced English reproduction furniture of all sorts and the firm flourished, supplying furniture to the Royal Family in 1933. Its production grew to include high quality modern boardroom furniture and it was granted a royal warrant in 1958, with Jack Beresford, the son of Julius (and also an Olympic sculler), named as the grantee.

In 1967 the Greater London Council purchased the Hemsworth Street factory, and a new factory was erected at Kings Lynn. At about this time the firm merged with Alfred Cox of Corsham Street, N1, another old-established, but ailing firm, and together they produced mainly modern domestic furniture.

The firm was acquired in 1972 by Uniflex, a firm itself formed as L. Lazarus & Sons by an immigrant with six sons who followed him into furniture manufacturing. Uniflex in turn was incorporated into the Christie-Tyler group, but ceased to exist in 1995.

D. Bianco & Sons (Immigration 1873)
This firm was established in 1880 by Domenico Bianco, a Roman Catholic who came from Piedmont in Italy in 1873. It started off as a small workshop in the basement of his house, just off Tottenham Court Road, London.

Bianco was making furniture of a very high quality in French and Italian period styles, as well as in the English styles produced by most of the other immigrants. By 1913 he had built a steel and concrete building in Chenies Street, off Tottenham Court Road, in the West End of London. He had been joined by his sons Mario and Silvio in the early 1900's and the firm then became D. Bianco & Sons. The company was engaged on government work in both World Wars. After the Second World War the firm continued making high grade furniture and panelling etc. for individual customers in a small factory in Camden Town, and eventually merged with the competing firm of Charles Pegram in the 1980's. The last member of the family working in the company, Lionel Bianco, died recently, having expressed great interest in my historical survey of immigrant furniture-makers.

D. Bürkle & Sons (Immigration 1874)
Philip David Bürkle was a Christian immigrant from Schmiden, near Würtemberg in South Germany, who arrived in London in 1874. At the time of his arrival, he was a married man of 30 with two children. By 1881 he had established his own business at 138 Hampstead Road, NW1, near the Tottenham Court Road retailers who were probably among his first customers. He was naturalized in 1884, by which time seven children were noted on the certificate.

His sons, Charles and Richard, joined the business in 1887, and, by

1896, the company already employed approximately 100 staff. The impressive, bound catalogue of 1900 illustrates a very wide range of Rococo-style furniture, highly carved and ornamented, which clearly shows German design influence. It became the anglicized 'D. Burkle & Sons Ltd' in 1907, and the company moved frequently around the Euston area as it grew, until it finally settled in Elthorne Road, Holloway, in 1929.

During the First World War the company had worked for the Admiralty, and during the Second World War it produced aircraft and shell cases, at that time employing 150-200 staff. Between the wars, the firm started manufacturing high quality specialist joinery such as panelling and bank fittings, which they then produced together with English-style reproduction furniture of high quality, which was made in small batches, and sold through exclusive retailers throughout the country or via specifying architects. David and Robert Burkle constituted the fourth working generation of the family in the firm, but, owing to various recessions, the firm was unable to carry on competitively and ceased production in 1992.

Burkle and Bianco seem to have been the only substantial firms which emerged from the immigrants who settled and worked in the "West End" area around Tottenham Court Road. By the 1920's, however, Burkle seems to have been employing mainly English workers (with a sprinkling of Germans), whilst Bianco at that time employed very few English people, concentrating on Italians, French, Germans, Belgians, Dutchmen and Poles.

Beautility (Immigration 1885)

This business was started by Simon Sadovsky in 1896 in Shoreditch. He had arrived from Russia in 1885 and probably worked for Harris Lebus or some other firms in the interim. His output in his own business, when he started on his own, was mainly English Period furniture in mahogany and walnut.

He was later joined by his three sons, Ronald, Gerald and Harvey. Ronald, the eldest, went to evening classes to learn technical drawing and furniture design. Gerald went to the U.S.A. to study modern production methods, and Harvey concentrated on publicity, advertising and marketing. By 1927 the firm had moved to a larger factory at Scawfell Street, Hackney Road, still making fine Period furniture. Simon died in January 1930 at the age of 65, and by the summer of that year the three sons felt able to move to a specially built, spacious, single-storey factory at Angel Road, Edmonton. The firm adopted the brand-name of "Beautility", which Harvey had created, and production included tables, sideboards and dining chairs. It became a public company in 1935, one of the first formed by companies with East End roots.

On the outbreak of war in 1939, the firm turned to producing a vast range of wood products required for the war effort such as ammunition boxes, tent equipment and institutional furniture. After the war, standardized Utility furniture was made until "Freedom of Design" was permitted in November 1948, at which time they returned to producing their own designs.

The firm continued to prosper, and Ronald and Gerald retired in 1957, Harvey having died at the early age of 39 after distinguished war service. The firm was purchased by Isaac Wolfson's G.U.S. group, then was passed on to Bowater's who sold it together with the name "Beautility" to F. Austin (op cit) for just £1. It terminated with Austinsuite in 1982.

Most of the facts regarding this company were provided by Lily, the youngest and last survivor from Simon's seven children. Lily was married to Jack Summers, whose father had started as a woodturner and had developed a substantial company making good quality oak dining suites.

Sklan (Immigration 1887)
This firm was started by Isaac Jacob Sklanowitz only two years after his arrival from East Poland in 1887. He was trained as a carpenter, but he must have been highly skilled as by the age of 25 he was producing high quality bedroom and dining suites in English Period styles. Within a relatively short time he was supplying firms like Harrods, Maples and Waring & Gillow. He was joined by his eldest son Solomon in 1902, and by two younger sons as the business progressed. Solomon took over when his father died in 1914.

The firm progressed to a four-storey building in Tabernacle Street, London EC2, and later moved to Old Ford when Solomon's son, Jack Sklan, took over. The firm ceased to exist in the 1960's. Jack, from whom I received most of the details on the firm, resides at the time of writing in Jerusalem.

Ducal (Immigration 1890)
Isaac Wiseman set up in business as a cabinet maker and retailer in Cambridge Heath Road, E2 in about 1900, having arrived from Czernowitz, Romania, ten years earlier. His son Sydney (born 1902) started his own business in Ducal Street, E2 as Ducal Woodware (1943) Ltd, making domestic woodware and small household items.

Sydney's son, Jeffrey, born in 1935, joined him in 1955 after studying as an accountant. Sydney, diabetic and with heart trouble, died in 1969, but Jeffrey had already assumed responsibility in 1960. The business moved several times quite quickly, finishing up at the Isle of Dogs in 1972.

The production of solid pine cabinet furniture started in 1966 when Jeffrey was walking down Regent Street one Thursday afternoon with his wife, and noticed an old pine dresser as part of a window display at Liberty's department store. He said: " I think that's an idea," and within four weeks the first samples of bedroom furniture were produced. He told me that he lost £30,000 in the first six months of production, for two reasons: the retail trade was suspicious of the use of softwood for this type of furniture, and the furniture which was sold then became warped or split in the furniture showrooms because the timber used was unseasoned.

In spite of this disastrous start, Jeffrey's instincts told him to persist even against the apparent logic of the situation, and the company then began to learn about kilning and handling timber. Thus, today Ducal is the major producer of pine furniture in this country. It accounts for one eighth of national production (*The Cabinet Maker* of 21st February 1997), and is indeed probably the largest producer of pine furniture in Europe. Due to its success in developing this market, many imitators have followed their lead in producing this type of furniture.

Additional factory space was taken in Andover, Hampshire in 1983, by which time pine had been accepted in the market generally. A. Younger Ltd, a furniture manufacturer long established in the same town, then failed, and Ducal purchased their factory and plant. Since then, there has been continuous expansion there, and, at the time of writing, the company has ten factories operating in Andover with a total floor space of about 350,000 sq. ft.

The firm's output now exceeds £1 million per week, with timber consumption - all pine seasoned by kilning and wrapped for protection against the hazards of the elements - averaging 25 cubic metres per day. The pine used comes only from Finland and

Sweden, and is ecologically sound in that every tree felled is replaced by three new saplings. From the original designs for bedroom use, products now serve every room in the house including specialist furniture for home entertainment and computers.

It seems to me that pine furniture is a significant development of the late 20th century, since previously the use of pine in furniture was restricted to kitchens and servants' quarters, with hardwood solids and veneers being used in all other areas. The furniture trade believes its use will now continue well into the 21st century (*The Cabinet Maker op cit*) and Ducal's exports all over the world are growing.

I asked Jeffrey Wiseman the philosophy behind this sensational development, which he explained as threefold: firstly, it is generally more economical to purchase pine than the traditional mahogany, walnut, teak and rosewood furniture; secondly, it is "solid" timber, rather than the normal veneered particle board with solid edges, and, thirdly, it is ecologically acceptable.

His comments on "solid timber" complete for me a one hundred year cycle. Lebus, at the turn of the century, with the largest production in Europe, was using only solid timber, before the arrival of plywood, chipboard, flaxboard and MDF. Ercolani, from the mid-1950's, was using solid elm and beech. John Makepeace, like other craft furniture makers from the 1960's onwards, was using mainly solid timber for his unique designs and unusual furniture, albeit produced in much smaller quantities. Now, Ducal is producing vast quantities of furniture, again using only solid timber with plywood backs and drawer-bottoms.

Unusually, upholstery was added to the range of furniture

production in 1989, and an additional factory was added in South Wales for this purpose. The total labour force is currently 850 and planned to reach 1,000 by the year 2000.

The story of Ducal's rapid growth at the end of the twentieth century, after decades of unspectacular existence, is unparalleled in the UK furniture industry, and Jeffrey's sons, James and Simon, now management trainees, constitute a fourth generation of this remarkable firm.

H & L Epstein (Immigration 1890)

Morris Epstein arrived from somewhere in Russia in 1890, and set up in business on his own account in 1913 in Gun St, E1, making high class furniture. He was joined by his six sons as soon as they left school and trained them as skilled cabinet makers.

One son formed a firm known as Epstein & Goldman, and two sons, Harry and Lewis, formed H & L Epstein in 1935 which moved to Hanbury Street near Brick Lane in the 1950's. The furniture produced by both firms was mainly made to order in heavily carved reproduction styles, and finished in highly figured burr walnut - sometimes bleached - or in bird's eye maple. Production included dining room suites and cocktail cabinets, bedroom furniture and, unusually, upholstered suites. However, H. & L. Epstein, developed into a much larger firm than Epstein & Goldman, employing eighty workers at their peak, and became well known from the 1950's as suppliers to affluent Jewish families.

The firm closed in 1986 after the death of Lewis Epstein, and I understand that all benches, cramps, glue-pots, records and photographs were donated to the Geffrye Museum upon the demise of the company. I am also told that a small collectors' market exists today in some of their pieces.

D & J Simons (Immigration 1891)
Davis Simons arrived in London in 1891 at the age of seventeen. He had been apprenticed as a woodturner in Warsaw, and his brother Morris was already here. Davis worked as a journeyman woodturner for a period and hired a lathe in Hive's Mill, Bacon Street, but only set up his own business with his own plant in rented premises, living above the shop in Virginia Road, E2. He moved to Hackney Road in 1922, and the firm has occupied a prime position up to this day. He was joined by his son, Jack, in 1930, who now has three sons in the business.

The business has grown enormously over the generations, now supplying the furniture and D.I.Y.trades with legs, mouldings. plywood, etc in large quantities. The bulk of the business is now in imported picture-frame mouldings of which they carry an enormous stock, while a small quantity of production is still carried out nearby. The firm recently acquired the large premises next door which previously belonged to the old-established firm of William Mallinson & Sons, veneer merchants, and I am advised that a fourth generation of Simons, currently students, are destined to continue working in the firm.

Mitchell & Barnet (Immigration 1891)
Barnet Abrahams was brought to London as a one-year old child in 1891 and probably went to Jews' Free School until 1904. He learnt his trade in East End workshops, and in the Great War worked on the construction of Army huts and in war work, possibly in the Harris Lebus factory.

In 1920, he joined a Mr Mitchell to form the firm of Mitchell & Barnet, specializing in china cabinets and bookcases in Hoxton Market quite close to my own firm in Coronet Street. During the Second World War, under a government initiative called

"Concentration of Industry", his firm was amalgamated with I. Abel & Son in Hertford Road N1, to make Utility furniture until 1948. The firm then went back to producing china cabinets and became one of the largest firms in this market in the East End. Barnet Abrahams retired in 1955 and joined his son Gerald, who had formed the firm of Universal Fittings (Kingsland) Ltd in Hackney Road, E2. Barnet Abrahams then assisted Gerald in building Universal into one of the leading suppliers of fittings and fixings to the furniture and allied trades in the U.K.

Stonehill Furniture (Immigration 1895)
Nathan Steinberg arrived here, aged 13, in 1895 from Tarnopol in Austria. He worked as an apprentice cabinet maker and commenced business on his own account in 1910, making bedroom furniture. The company became Stonehill Furniture after the Second World War, and became a public company in 1964. The main factory was in Angel Factory Colony at Edmonton in North London, but several other factories were in the group including a former Co-op. factory in Pelaw, Co. Durham.

By the 1980's Stonehill was among the largest furniture firms in Great Britain, producing mainly dining room furniture. Nathan's sons, Philip and Maurice Steinberg, ran the business up to the 1980's until their retirement.

J. Cinnamon/ "Cintique" (Immigration 1896)
Jack Cinnamon came to London in 1896 at the age of nine, apparently without his parents. After leaving school at the age of fourteen, he went to work for W. G. Tagg, upholsterer of Old Ford, where he was trained as a chair-frame maker. He married in 1914 and, at the same time, set up in Dalston, E8, as a maker of chair-frames (to be upholstered by others) and of complete dining chairs. This was rather unusual since, at that time, most of the dining

chairs were supplied by the traditional makers in High Wycombe and sold together with tables, sideboards etc., produced in the East End.

He moved to Andrews Road, Cambridge Heath, in the early 1920's; this factory became known as Firmback Works and is still in production at the time of writing. Jack Cinnamon died in 1932 and the business was then run by his daughter, Rita Lee, wife of Jack Lee of the furniture-factoring firm of N. Lee & Sons. Later the company was run by her two brothers, Lionel and Ellis Cinnamon, and their furniture was sold under the brand name of "Cintique". Lionel, the older brother died in 1979, and the business was then run very successfully by his widow, Jacqueline, until it was sold to Silentnight, a very large bedding manufacturer based in the North of England, in 1988.

F. Austin/"Austinsuite" (Immigration 1898)
An immigrant called Ornstein arrived in London in 1898 from Austria and worked for various firms. He then went to Plymouth in the first decade of the century, and set up as a bamboo furniture maker - surely the only Jewish bamboo furniture-maker in the country? He then returned to London and died at an early age in 1914. His son Frank, whose surname had been anglicized to Austin, together with three brothers, Nat, Sam and Lewis, and later with a brother-in-law, Cyril Salkind, set up in a very small workshop in Stamp Place off Shoreditch High Street in 1928. By 1936 they had expanded into a factory of no less than 35,000 sq.ft. in Leyton specializing in modern and traditional bedroom suites under the trade-name of "Austinsuite".

During the Second World War the company was engaged in government contracts of various kinds including aircraft repairs. After the War in 1948, it became a public company and developed rapidly into one of the leading furniture manufacturers in its field. The factory at Leyton was expanded to 400,000 sq. ft. and employed 650 people by 1978, fifty years after its foundation. The company then merged with the ailing firm of Beautility (see above), but the whole firm was wound up in 1982. In 1987 after the demise of Austinsuite, Frank Austin was invited to give a talk on his association with the trade, under the auspices of the Jewish Historical Society of England, to coincide with the Geffrye Museum's exhibition "Furnishing the World: the East End Furniture Trade 1830 to 1980". His son, John, set up making contract furniture on a relatively small scale in Hertfordshire.

Frank Austin himself was an assertive character in business, and was also always active in the wider furniture industry and in local communal affairs. He thus helped to set up the Worshipful Company of Furniture Makers in the 1950s of which he served as Master in 1974-5. He also became National President of the Furniture Trades Benevolent Association and was appointed a magistrate in 1951 in Walthamstow and sat on the London Bench from 1969 to 1976. He founded the Waltham Forest branch of the Citizens' Advice Bureau and became its first chairman.

Lucas Furniture Systems (Immigration 1898)
This firm was founded by Jack Lubelsky in Columbia Road in the East End of London, following his arrival in London in 1898 from Grodno in Russia, where he had been in the army making furniture for army officers and their wives. According to family account, as soon as he arrived in London he immediately started in business, producing large work-tables for garment-workers in East London. As he was highly skilled, he also proved able to obtain orders quickly for bedroom-suites from prestigious firms such as Maples and Waring & Gillow in London, and Wylie & Lockhead in Glasgow.

1. B. Cohen & Sons Ltd, 1-19 Curtain Road, London, EC2. Advertisement in *The Cabinet Maker*, June 1904. *Photo Studios, courtesy of the Geffrye Museum.*

2. The woodwork class at the Jews' Free School, London, 1908.
Courtesy of London Metropolitan Archive.

3. Lebus polishing shop, 1912.
Courtesy of the Lebus Archives, Victoria and Albert Museum.

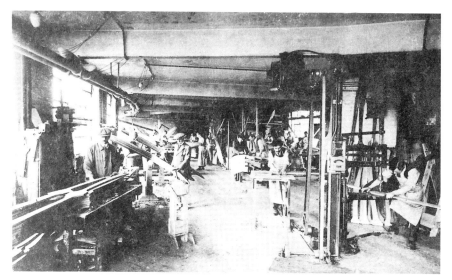

4. Interior of D. Bianco and Sons' workshop at Chenies Street, off Tottenham Court Road, London W1. During the First World War the firm made propellors.

5. Exterior of D. Bianco and Sons'showrooms at Chenies Street, London W1 with father, grandfather and uncle standing outside.
Jewish Museum London, courtesy of Roy Bianco.

6. Two Chinese Chippendale style chairs designed by Mrs Ray Hille, 1920. This range of furniture formed a bridge between strict reproduction style and the more fanciful forms of Art Deco. *Courtesy of Hille International Ltd.*

7. James Latham Ltd, 120 Curtain Road, EC2, c 1920. James Latham was one of East London's largest and most reputable timber merchants for over 150 years. In the 1920's they moved from their premises in Curtain Road to Lea Bridge Wharf, Clapton, where they are still in operation today. *Courtesy of the Geffrye Museum and James Latham Ltd.*

8.Employees of Nathan Leibovitch, cabinet makers, 29-31 Hoxton Square, on a charbanc outing, 1923. *London Borough of Hackney Archives Department.*

9. Shop exterior of I. Wiseman, General Cabinetmaker and Household Furnisher, at 489 Cambridge Heath Road, London E2, 1924. Isaac Wiseman (wearing a cap) was born in 1875 and is standing with with Sydney Wiseman (born 1902) and Hetty and Jeanie Wiseman. The firm later became Ducal Ltd. *The Jewish Museum London, courtesy of Jeffrey Wiseman.*

10. From left to right: Nat, Frank, Lew and Sam Austin in a photograph dated 1928, outside the original premises of their cabinetmaking firm at 1-3 French Place, Shoreditch. Reproduced from *The Cabinetmaker and Retail Furnisher,* December 1, 1978. This firm was to become the well-known company Austinsuite.

11. Mrs Ray Hille in workshop with carver, 1935. *Courtesy of Hille International Ltd.*

12. A mahogany "break-front" bookcase made by Hille, 1946-47.
Courtesy of Hille International Ltd.

13. Lebus, Finsbury Works, Tottenham, London N17. Advertisement for Utility furniture, *The Cabinet Maker and Complete Household Furnisher*, 19 July 1947. *Photo Studios, courtesy of the Geffrye Museum.*

14. Lebus factory, Ferry Lane, Tottenham, London N17, 1947.
Courtesy of Vestry House Museum, London.

15. Formed plywood chair, 1951. Made by S. Hille & Co of Lea Bridge
Road, Leyton, London E10. *Courtesy of Hille International Ltd.*

16. Ducal Place, off Brick Lane, where the firm of Ducal Ltd originated.
Courtesy of London Metropolitan Archive and Godfrey New Photograp

17. Recent photograph of part of Ducal's factory at Andover, Hampshire.
The size of the factory is 350,000 sq.ft. *Courtesy of Jeffrey Wiseman.*

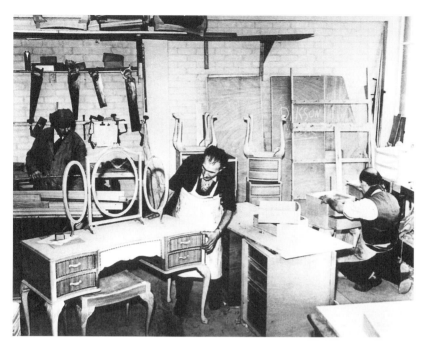

18. Cabinet making workshops, Long Street, London E2. 1955.
London Metropolitan Archive.

19. Epstein's furniture factory, February 1955 . One of the woodcarvers at
work. *Photograph by Ronald Chapman, courtesy of the Geffrye Museum.*

20. Photograph of Arnold Herman Barmaper, a Jewish timber merchant from Austria, in his timber yard in Bethnal Green with two workers. *The Jewish Museum, London.*

The original firm became J. Lubelsky & Sons, as his sons joined him and moved out from Columbia Road to Old Ford in Bethnal Green. After the Second World War its name changed to Palatial Furniture, and, for a time, the company gained fame by refining its production down to only one design of bedroom furniture. Later, the name of the company was changed to Lucas Furniture Systems, reflecting a change in marketing to high-quality office furniture. The firm was taken over at some time in the 1980's and the Lubelsky/Lucas family connection was terminated.

Gabe & Pass (Immigration 1898)

Bernard Gabe, a woodcarver, arrived here from Odessa in the Ukraine in 1898. He set up in business with a Mr Pass, his brother-in-law, who was reputed to have been a very fine designer, but died young. The firm was always run on a small scale, producing the highest quality furniture in English Period styles, and received special recognition at an exhibition in Brussels in 1925. Bernard Gabe then continued production of high quality furniture for Maples, Waring & Gillow and the major retailers all over Britain. During his retirement in the 1950's, Mr Gabe had *carte blanche* from Maples and similar firms to purchase secondhand furniture of the highest quality on their behalf.

Ercol Furniture (Immigration 1898)

Luciano Ercolani arrived here from Tuscany, Italy, in 1898 at the age of 10. His father, a cabinet maker, had converted in Florence from Roman Catholicism to the Baptist rite with leanings towards the Salvation Army. He had produced work for the Uffizi Gallery in Florence and was apparently the only craftsman who could make a special kind of oval frame which the gallery required.

Luciano, after leaving school in England, had various jobs in woodworking including being a carpenter at the Salvation Army's depot at Queen Victoria Street in London. He attended evening classes at Shoreditch Technical Institute, which later became the London College of Furniture, and studied there with Percy Wells and Mr Hooper who both became very well-known in the industry later in the early 1930's. His *forte* seems to have been furniture design because in 1910 he was asked by Frederick Parker, whose firm in High Wycombe later became famous as Parker Knoll, to join him as a designer. Here, as Ercolani recalls in his autobiography *A Furniture Maker* the factory was "dark, untidy and disorderly", but the men were making what he described as the "jewellery of furniture."

After three or four years at Parker's, he was befriended by the Gomme family, and worked in the family firm of Ebenezer Gomme, later to become well known as the manufacturers of "G-Plan Furniture".

His big breakthrough occurred at the age of 32 when he secured finance and support from a small group of businessmen with no connections in the furniture trade, who nonetheless put up the significant sum of £10,000 in order that he could purchase a five acre site in High Wycombe to build his own factory, thus forming the firm of Furniture Industries Ltd in 1920. There he manufactured middle quality traditional furniture and later acquired the old established local firm of Walter Skull, which was experiencing financial difficulties and was involved in higher quality production which he continued.

During the Second World War he was engaged in wood-based war contracts of every kind. After the war, when his sons, Lucian and Barry, returned from distinguished war service, he was able to put into practice a lifetime's experience by creating a completely new range of furniture. This range was constructed out of solid elm and beech, and uniquely combined modern design with the simplicity of the "Arts and Crafts" movement and a feeling for the traditional oak furniture he had previously produced. In my opinion his main contribution was unique in visual design and in technical construction. He transformed the use of home-grown elm - until then the "Cinderella" of British hardwoods - from cheap wood, prone to distortion during seasoning and used mainly for coffin construction, to a beautifully figured timber used constructionally in perfect combination with beech-turned legs and rails. By now the firm was trading as Ercol Furniture Ltd and apparently employed about 1,000 individuals with its products exported to many countries of the world including Japan.

High Wycombe had been for two or three centuries the traditional home of English chair-making using locally grown beech gathered from the woods in the surrounding countryside. Ercolani must have had a difficult journey, as apparently the only immigrant furniture maker working in such a conservative area, but he was certainly successful in engraving his name in the annals of British furniture through great abilities and creativity in design, manufacturing and construction. The company is still flourishing at the time of writing, in contrast to many of the formerly great firms of the industry, and its ownership is still held in family hands. It is also worth noting that Luciano's brother, Vittorio Ercolani, arrived in England with him and was also very successful in setting up a large company, later known as Cabinet Industries Ltd in Chingford, making wooden radio and television cabinets in vast quantities.

Peter Waals (Immigration 1899)

Born Peter van der Waals in the Netherlands in 1870, Waals learned his trade as a cabinet maker in the Netherlands, Belgium, Germany and Austria from 1885 before reaching London in 1899, where he remained until 1901. His skills must have been at an extremely high level since he was then accepted to work for Ernest Gimson, no less in the Cotswolds. Gimson, newly established at that time in a peaceful workshop at Sapperton with the Barnsley brothers, eight horse-drawn miles from Cirencester, stood as the heir and chief protagonist of the Arts and Crafts tradition of John Ruskin and William Morris, and his bucolic workshop, using only hand tools, must have presented a stark contrast to the commercially driven and increasingly mechanized enterprises at which most new immigrants found work at the time.

Gimson in fact was a designer not a craftsman, and Waals stayed with him for nineteen years as chief cabinet maker. Sir George Trevelyan, in his "Tribute from a Pupil", states that, though a young man on arrival, Waals worked from the outset in the closest cooperation with Gimson in checking and discussing designs and construction. "The association of these two men was an essential factor in the evolving of the Cotswold Tradition", he says, and the intricate inlay and octagonal fielding characteristic of Gimson's later work were attributed to Waals.

After Gimson's death in 1919, Waals - less purist than his master had been - moved into an old woollen mill close to a railway siding at Chalford near Stroud where he installed simple woodworking machinery. Here he produced many one-off pieces of very high quality craftsmanship and refinement using both his own as well as some of Gimson's old designs. Trevelyan describes Waals as generally of forbidding personality except when talking about his craft, yet many of his fellow-craftsmen came with him from Gimson's workshop.

In 1935 he was appointed Design Adviser to Loughborough College to promote good design in schools at the recommendation of Frank Pick, well known for his design work on the London Underground In 1935 he died at Chalford and the following year a fire at Waals' workshops destroyed nearly all his own and probably many of Gimson's designs, while he was succeeded at Loughborough by Edward Barnsley.

S. Hille (Immigration 1900)
This firm was started by Salomon Hille who arrived in London from the Ukraine in 1900. Not a cabinet maker, his first job here was apparently managing a firm of wine merchants. He was, however, very interested in historic furniture and spent much of his spare time at the Victoria & Albert and other museums, studying the details of English Period furniture. He also visited their libraries and became familiar with the great body of English cabinet and furniture-making pattern books, such as those produced by Chippendale, Hepplewhite and Sheraton.

By 1906 he had turned his hobby to practical effect by employing a cabinet maker and a wood-carver in a small workshop in Rutland Street, Whitechapel. Here he was to produce fine furniture for the home he was preparing for his wife and two daughters who were soon to follow him to England.
He then left the wine business and set up in earnest in a larger workshop in Derbyshire Street in Bethnal Green together with several more men. The business must have flourished because by the time of the Great War in 1914 the company employed 80 workers including cabinet makers, carvers and apprentices.

Hille's main output for his first four years was English Period furniture for stores like Hampton's, Maples and Waring & Gillow, and for wealthy private clients. By the 1930's the business had established an international reputation, and a fair amount was exported to Australia and other parts of the British Empire and to the United States.

Salomon's daughter, Ray, had joined him as a part-time designer in the 1920's although she was also employed by the Civil Service. By 1932, owing to ill health, Salomon decided to retire and handed over the running of the firm to Ray. At that time it was quite unusual for a woman to run a substantial furniture-manufacturing business. The main exception to this was Betty Joel, who set up her own company in the 1920's to make Art Deco furniture to her design. This continued up to the Second World War. Ray Hille also produced Art Deco at this time, together with "Hollywood", modified Bauhaus and International Style designs. She also developed Chinese lacquer work on the traditional Chippendale-type furniture.

Salomon died in retirement in 1940, and, soon after, the works were completely destroyed by fire together with all the plant, valuable stocks of timber, veneer etc and all records of designs and customers. During the Second World War, Ray continued with a small staff of skilled men, repairing high quality bomb-damaged furniture for insurance companies and City institutions by recommendation from a curator of the Victoria and Albert Museum. After the war, factory premises were taken in Lea Bridge Road in Clapton, and she was joined by her husband Maurice, and subsequently by her daughters Cheryl and Rosamind, together with Rosamind's husband, Leslie Julius, who had trained as a surveyor.

Initially, the firm continued its tradition of producing high grade reproduction furniture, much of which was exported. However, in 1949 the Julius's invited Robin Day, an award-winning English designer, to join the firm, after they had become attracted to modern design during their frequent selling trips to North America. Day was to have a dramatic influence on the development of the firm until the 1970's and his modern designs for letterheads, forms, vehicle livery as well as for all sorts of furniture using shaped plywood, metal and other non-traditional materials and forms, were to take over completely. The use of Hille's furniture throughout the Royal Festival Hall in 1951 gave the firm wide publicity and they then moved to larger premises in North Watford.

In 1981, the Victoria and Albert Museum mounted an exhibition with an elaborate catalogue by Sutherland Lyall called *"Hille - 75 years of British Furniture"*, which I believe to have been the first to illustrate the birth and history of a contemporary manufacturing company. In 1984 the business was sold to Ergonom, a metal furniture manufacturing company who changed its name to Hille-Ergonom, and with whom Cheryl continued working as designer for a few years, after which the family connection ended.

Arenson Group (Immigration 1903)
Solomon Arenson arrived in London in 1903 from Ula near Vitebsk in Russia at the age of 24. After working for several employers in the East End, he started his own business in 1919 making oak bureaux, bookcases and sideboards.

Archy, the youngest of his six children, was born in 1926, but the father died in 1941 when Archy was only fifteen. After evacuation as a schoolboy in the war years, Archy went to technical colleges and evening classes to learn engineering, and then worked at Napiers' in Acton as a trainee engineer.

In 1949 he established his own company in Holloway Road, N19, making tables out of tubular steel with Formica tops - non-traditional materials which capitalized on his engineering background. These formed "dinette" and "kitchenette" suites which were sold to retailers such as John Lewis and Woolfe & Hollander.

A few years later he moved to a small factory estate in Barnet, and conceived the idea of the the first "knock-down" office furniture in the UK. The business was then growing very rapidly and moved to a purpose-built factory near St Albans in 1960. This factory immediately suffered a disastrous fire, but Archy, always known as a man of great integrity, was helped by friends in the trade to re-establish production, where he continued to manufacture kitchen and other domestic furniture in the fashion of the time.

For some time he was trying to diversify his product range, but, according to his obituary in *The Cabinet Maker* of November 12 1993, " the night before the opening of the 1964 Earls Court furniture show, he decided to concentrate on what was to become President Office Furniture with the Lincoln and Columbus ranges." This proved to be a very successful decision, as it initiated great commercial success, which rapidly led to the final re-development of the firm to become a very sophisticated, 240,000 sq ft factory and it was successfully launched as a public company in 1970. The company then concentrated on complete modern office desking systems generally in timber finishes, together with metal-based office seating, sold in large quantities to both home and export markets.

In 1988 the company was purchased by Skandinavisk Holding of Copenhagen, with Archy staying on as non-executive director until his death five years later. In his semi-retirement he increased his involvement with ORT, an international, Jewish-based charity concerned with re-training and technology for young people, of which he became Chairman from 1988 to 1992, and to which he made very generous endowments.

I am pleased to record the story of the Arenson organization since it became rapidly, and remains, pre-eminent in the field of office furniture in the UK, and, at the time of writing in July 1997, I understand that a further move has just been made into a still larger factory with ultra-modern equipment at Dunstable.

Massils of Marshmoor (Immigration 1905)

My father, Hyman Massil, came to London in 1905 from a village in Byelorussia called Azarich. He must have been a skilled woodturner as he found a job very quickly at a well established firm called Franklin & Goldberg in Hackney Road, Shoreditch. In a very short time he became the foreman. However in 1912 or thereabouts he decided to set up on his own, nearby in a workshop in Coronet Street in Shoreditch, and opened a bank account at Barclays, Great Eastern Street at the same time.

It may be worth mentioning at this point that it would have been much more difficult to set up as a woodturner than as a cabinet maker. The latter could start with a bench and tools in a small workshop - no machinery would have been required and any "rough" machining such as sawing, planing etc would be done for him in a local Trade Mill of which there were several at that time in the East End of London. In contrast, a woodturner would have needed machinery such as lathes, boring machines and other simple plant. There would have been a whole panoply of shafts, counter-shafts and pulleys, powered by electric motors, all of which would have needed considerable capital and space.

My father's brother, Morris, must have joined him later in the early part of the First World War, as I can still remember, as a small child about 1916 or 1917, the caption on the fascia of the workshop "H & M Massil, Woodturners and Twisters". The "twisting" presumably referred to the Jacobean twists or barley-sugar legs, stretchers and columns which were made for reproductions of the 17th century Jacobean pieces that were very popular at that time, and subsequently into the 1920's and 1930's.

Hyman Massil must have found his customer among the small cabinet makers and upholsterers who abounded in the area of

Curtain Road, Great Eastern Street and Hackney Road and in the many side-turnings that existed.

By the time I joined him in the late 1920's, he had built up a fairly large clientèle, providing as well as turnings for furniture makers, columns and finials for the elaborate cases used by the high quality clockmakers from the Clerkenwell area, who were all non-Jewish and often of Italian origin. Customers included firms with Dickensian names like Peckover & Spinks, or Puddefoot, Simonett and Bower, who had in fact amalgamated with John Betjeman's father's firm, and who made small ornate timber-based pieces for elegant firms like Asprey's.

As my father was basically a craftsman, and a very fine one at that, within a year or two I found myself running the commercial end of the business, such as it was. We were going through the Depression of the early 1930's, and cashflow - or lack of cashflow - was a constant problem. However by 1938/9 we had moved to larger premises in Hoxton Street, and had even installed a second-hand automatic turning machine by Guilliet of Brussels, the use of which no longer required skilled woodturners.

Fortuitously, equipped with this machine, when war broke out in 1939 we were able to approach the Ministry of Supply regarding the production of turnings for war contracts. The Ministry needed tool handles, ladder rungs, tent components and a whole range of items which we produced from blueprints; in some cases we did not even know of their intended ultimate use. The items for war contracts were sometimes required in enormous quantities, in contrast to the traditional retail-oriented manufacturers, who required relatively small batches. Continually stopping work due to the need to rush down into air raid shelters became tiresome to all concerned, and, after a little while, it was resolved to carry on working in the factory through the air raids, and to hope for the best. In fact, the war was survived with minimal damage.

The firm had meanwhile obtained a whole range of woodturning machinery - all old and battered, and, in some cases, primitive, but it was clearly time to take stock and plan for the future. While this obviously lay with the furniture trade, at that time production was limited to Utility Furniture where the only turnery was wooden knobs for chests of drawers."Freedom of Design" (whereby manufacturers could make whatever furniture they wished) was a long way off and we had to wait until November 1948 before the market could take the full range of furniture products which had been produced before the war.

At this time we moved to very much larger premises with a railway siding called Marshmoor, at Welham Green in Hertfordshire. There were 30,000 to 40,000 square feet of ramshackle buildings on a four acre site. There were also timber sheds and ample space for the erection of drying kilns which we considered absolutely essential for the building-up of an efficient unit for mass-produced wood turnery. In due course modern turnery plant was introduced, including copying lathes for eccentric turnery such as "Queen Anne" or cabriole legs, as well as items like pick-axe handles, rifle-butts etc. By 1959 a modern factory of 50,000 square feet was in place with an office block and 14 large drying kilns which could cope with about 4,000 cubic feet of beech "squares" per week, in a whole range of lengths and thicknesses.

The business was disposed of in 1960 to an industrial conglomerate, and I stayed on as managing director until 1964. The firm then continued under the direction of Daniel Eckstein who had been the company's cost-accountant originally, and who bought the company himself in the early 1970's. At this time production levels fell and, with the decline of the British furniture industry, the firm diversified its market to supply new users of turned products such as Dr Scholl footwear and Marks and Spencers, who had started marketing small bathroom woodware items. Finally the business was sold to another Marks and Spencer supplier, Peter Black Ltd, and with the retirement of Mr Eckstein, production ceased in 1985 when the site was sold for development.

B. Serota & Sons (Immigration 1905)

Barnett Serota came to London from Zhitomir, Russia, in 1905. He was a maker of very high class furniture, and obtained a job with Morris Cohen, who ran a small furniture factory at that time and later became a veneer-merchant, and whose grandsons subsequently formed the innovative firm of Bonded Laminates.

In 1911, Serota set up with Nathan Cohen as Serota & Cohen, in Luke Street off Curtain Road, making high quality oak reproduction dining furniture and walnut and mahogany occasional furniture, later expanding to bedroom suites. They supplied retail shops, particularly in the North of England and Scotland.

The partnership was dissolved in 1924, when Serota's son Louis, joined him in a newly built factory in Downham Road, off Kingsland Road, on the edge of Shoreditch.

A younger son, Morris, joined the firm in 1939 at the age of 17, but was called up for RAF service in 1942, rejoining the firm in 1946. From 1942 to 1948 Utility dining tables and sideboards were produced, and, although the staff were highly skilled and not used to the semi-mass production of simple furniture, by introducing piece work or "payment by results" schemes, the firm was fairly successful and able to survive.

With "Freedom of Design" they reverted to their accustomed prewar quality and styles, but by the 1950's, with a purchase tax levy of 66%, their prices became prohibitive. They sought and obtained Ministry of Works contracts, such as laboratory furniture at Harwell, furniture for the Army and RAF, and specialist pieces for embassies abroad. In the early 1960s, they were approached by the Clerk of Works of London University to produce laboratory furniture. This venture led to a contract for a large library for the University's Institute of Education. In this way, they became specialists in the production of shelving, cupboards and desks for libraries, particularly for universities. Previously, Louis had designed all the domestic furniture produced and now applied his knowledge of construction to library furniture and fittings.

With the government freeze on spending in the 1980's, they were faced with problems of over-capacity in the industry and foreign competition. It was not thought possible to revert to domestic production, and production ceased in 1995.

Lebetkin Brothers (Immigration 1905)
Harris Lebetkin came to London from Grodno in Russia in 1905. He was a highly skilled cabinet maker, and worked for Isaac Griew until 1910, and for other firms until 1917 when he started on his own, making good quality solid oak bureaux and selling to wholesalers, no doubt in the Curtain Road area.

He was joined by his son Louis in 1922, at that time employing 12 skilled cabinetmakers. The firm moved to Darnley Road, Hackney in 1929, adding the production of dining room suites. A further move to Edmonton took place in 1934 where the skilled labour force had grown to 200. During the War they were involved in all types of government work.

The firm produced Utility furniture from 1945 until the advent of

"Freedom of Design" in November 1948. There was then a period of rapid growth. Thus Colover Brothers, a similar furniture manufacturer, was acquired in 1948; the associated firms of Maryland Furniture and E. Ritt, making much cheaper quality furniture, were acquired one year later, and a large production unit, Enfield Furniture Manufacturing Company, was purchased in 1950-51.

It seems, though, that there was over-expansion, and in 1957 the complete group was taken over by Schreiber (see below). At its peak, the Lebetkin Group had employed 1,500 people and Louis Lebetkin worked on until he retired in 1978. As far as I know, there is only one member of the family still in the furniture-manufacturing trade: Brian, Louis Lebetkin's son, who is running his own firm in the Cambridge Heath/Bethnal Green area, making occasional furniture.

Bluestone & Elvin (Immigration 1905)
Reuben Bluestone (possibly Blaustein?) came to London in 1905 from Lithuania at the age of 15. He very soon found a job at a firm called Elivitsky in the Bethnal Green area. He was related to the owners and, by 1919, they were in partnership as Bluestone & Elivitsky, which later became known as Bluestone & Elvin. The firm prospered and moved to a four-storey factory in Canal Road, off Kingsland Road, E2. By 1930 the firm had moved out to Walthamstow to a large, modern, single-storey factory. This must have been one of the first East End workshops to have moved to modern premises in the North London suburbs. The production during this period was solely bedroom suites, but by the 1950's they diversified into dining-room suites, and Massil's produced the turned legs for the first prototypes, and eventually for the full production.

A public company had been formed during the 1930's - again the first of its kind, apart from Harris Lebus, to emanate from an East End workshop. Dennis Bluestone, son of the founder, retired in 1982, and the business ceased production shortly thereafter.

The Serlin Family (Immigration 1905-10)
There were a number of immigrant families initially working together in the furniture trade who later split off into separate companies and the Serlin's were outstanding among them. Thus four brothers arrived here from Poland in the first decade of the century: Reuben in 1905, Lazarus in 1906, Joseph in 1908 and Gershon (later known as George) in 1910. They were a close-knit family, and all four joined together as a production unit in about 1910, working together until the First World War in 1914. Each one then became involved in war-work, either in factories, like Harris Lebus, or making army huts on Salisbury Plain.

After the War, they dispersed and formed four separate firms, each Serlin later being joined by their respective sons, and forming companies, all in and around Columbia Road, off Hackney Road.

The four firms were:

1) Validity Furniture Ltd, formed by Reuben, with a brand-name allegedly inspired by the name of his son Valentine, which specialized in heavy, oak, Jacobean-style dining furniture,

2) L. Serlin & Sons, making bedroom suites, china cabinets, etc.,

3) J. Serlin & Sons, making all sorts of domestic furniture to customers' requirements,

and:

4) G. Serlin & Sons who made upholstery as well as general domestic cabinet furniture. This firm eventually became known as Lancelot Furniture in the north-west London suburb of Mill Hill and was headed by Gershon's son, Morris. He became very successful in furniture delivered in flat-pack form for home-assembly by the customer.

All the Serlin firms except for Lancelot had ceased production at the date of writing, and as far as I know, there is now no member of the Serlin family still active in the trade.

Olympus Furniture (Immigration 1911)
This firm was started by Israel Bercovici who came to London from a village called Sevan in northern Romania in 1911. By 1912 he had started up in business in Vallance Road, Bethnal Green. After a series of moves around the East End, Curtain Road, Bethnal Green and Cambridge Heath, he settled in a fairly large factory (earlier occupied by Austinsuite) in Vyner Street in Cambridge Heath in 1950. His son, Gerry Burke, joined him in 1932, and their production was mainly of high quality 5 ft. and 6 ft bedroom suites, which were supplied to Nathan Steinberg (whose sons later formed Stonehill Furniture as noted above), and to retailers like Wolfe and Hollander in Tottenham Court Road. Their big move came in 1963 to a 100,000 sq ft factory in Lea Bridge Road, itself previously occupied by the Thermos flask organization.

Olympus Furniture is unusual in that it is one of the few firms of immigrant origin, which is still active in the business and is still run by Gerry with his son and son-in-law. Production consists of medium quality bedroom and dining room suites.

Alan Newman (Immigration 1914)
Baruch Newman was in England selling timber on behalf of the

Polish magnate, Count Potocki, when war broke out in 1914 and he was interned as an alien until 1918. He set up in business in a small workshop in Lambeth after the war, selling timber and making plywood and veneered panels, and sent for his wife and children who reached England. His son Alan (originally Aaron), worked for other companies in the same field and was involved in the wartime production of the plywood Mosquito bomber. In 1948 he set up in Finchley, retailing furniture and making one-off furniture and joinery for domestic use.

With the construction of new hotels and institutions in London of the 1960's, however, the company became heavily involved in manufacturing specialist furniture and joinery for the contract market. Alan Newman was joined by his son David in the late 1960's and moved into progressively larger factories around north London. The firm turned to overseas markets in the Middle East, Europe, Africa and the Caribbean, and production moved out of London to old-established furniture and joinery factories taken over in Dundee and Gosforth. With the recession of the late 1980's, however, the subsidiaries were sold off and the company closed.

Englender (Immigration 1923)

The 21-year old Samuel Englender came to London in 1923 from Yarov Padloçka, a village near Warsaw, and seems to have been one of the very few immigrants to arrive in the 1920s. He had previously only worked on a farm and had no previous working experience of the furniture trade. He went to work for his uncle, Mr Gordon, who was already established as an upholsterer in New nn Yard, Shoreditch, and, after work, attended evening classes to earn English.

Three years later, he set up independently in the same field with n English-born partner, Lionel Marks, with whom he had worked previously at Gordon's, as "Marks & Englender". After several moves, Englender was able to buy Mr Marks out for £1,370 in 1932, and set up on his own in the East End. He made high quality upholstery and sofas and became well known for a "fan back" lounge suite design, derived from the Shell Petrol sign, which the company manufactured into the 1950's. I can well remember his full-page advertisements in the trade press which he adorned with a Union Jack and the slogan: "There'll always be an Englender".

The firm developed up to 1939 when the business virtually came to a standstill through lack of materials and labour. In 1941 their premises in Leyton were requisitioned by the Ministry of Works, and most of the remaining workers were called up. With three or four older and part-time workers, the company survived on repairs to war-damaged upholstery under contract with the local council, and made a small amount of Utility upholstery thereafter.

In 1948, however, he purchased a partly destroyed 60,000 sq ft factory, previously used by Vickers, out in Weybridge, Surrey, where no skilled furniture labour was available. By the early 1950's, the company was thriving in its new location, producing upholstery sold into the retail market, and two sons, Norman and Michael joined the company. In 1958 the firm took up the production of expanded polystyrene chair shells in place of the traditional timber framed construction, and quickly became a leader in this field.

By 1973, the firm needed to expand further, and a 25 acre site was purchased next to the M1 motorway in Normanton in Derbyshire where they built initially a 100,000 sq ft factory.

In 1976 Sam Englender formally retired, and, with the demise of the many small, family-run retailers on which they had previously relied and the concurrent emergence of the "out of town" multiple discount warehouses, production started to expand into the contract field.

By 1985, it was resolved to withdraw entirely from the domestic furniture market and to concentrate on sales to the hotel and leisure contract market, for which the firm now also produces cabinet furniture. Two grandsons of the founder are now involved in the firm which also supplies many export markets, including Japan, and has diversified into producing cabinets and tables for the hospitality, health care and shipping markets.

H.K. Furniture (Immigration 1933)

Hans Krebs came here from Berlin in 1933 aged 31. He had been trading in Berlin as a textile merchant in the firm of Hart & Krebs, and set up Modern Tapestries Ltd in July 1933. He changed his name to Howard Keith and changed that of the company to H.K. Furniture Ltd in October of the same year, working from Kentish Town. The firm manufactured extremely high quality upholstered furniture, supplying Fortnum and Mason, Heal's, Bowman's and similar firms. Only two years after Mr Keith's arrival in Britain, his firm mounted a stand at the prestigious, export-orientated British Furniture Industry's exhibition. Indeed, an edition of *The Cabinet Maker* in February 1935 showed the august Queen Mary looking at a novel design for a convertible bed-settee on the HK stand, where she was quoted as saying: "It would be an amusing way to make anybody get up".

Production remained on a limited scale, however, until 1939 when war broke out. Howard Keith joined the Pioneer Corps, leaving the firm to be run by his wife and his English-born colleague, Joe Lawrence, who told me that Keith returned in 1944 when the firm moved to larger premises nearby.

Utility furniture was produced until 1948 when "Freedom of Design" was introduced into the furniture trade. Keith's strong points were furniture design and unusual fabrics whilst high quality was always predominant. As the business progressed much larger premises were taken in Hermitage Road, Haringey, where the firm is still thriving. Mrs Keith, also an immigrant, took a leading part in the business, working on the sewing-machines in wartime when necessary and taking over financial control as the firm progressed: they both retired in 1969. At some stage cabinet furniture such as sideboards, tables etc was introduced, also of a high quality, and today, the breakdown of production is 60% cabinet furniture and 40% upholstery.

Although never a large firm, it was always considered among the highest quality producers and modern designers in the trade.

Schreiber Wood Industries (Immigration 1938)
Chaim S. Schreiber, born in 1918, came to London from Lwow, Poland (formerly Lemburg) in May 1938. He had been studying architecture in Vienna, but with the *Anschluss* in March 1938, he decided it would be more comfortable to settle in England. His hobby was making marquetry pictures and, armed with some of these, he visited David Peskin of Austin Veneered Panel Company in Bethnal Green. The story may be apocryphal but my son-in-law's father, Alan Newman, recounted that he interpreted Schreiber's Yiddish to the Peskins when he came to their office to try to sell his very accomplished work. He kept going in this way until war broke out, supplying stores like Harrods.

During the Second World War, he worked for De Havilland, helping to produce wooden aircraft wings for aircraft like Mosquitoes. He commenced his own business in 1944, Lordship Products in Tottenham, supplying picture frames to various stores. With the coming of peace, he quickly set up in the radio/TV industry producing what became known as "wrap-round" plywood cabinet for firms such as Sobell, known as Radio and Allied Industries. In the 1950's he set up on a larger scale, first in Stevenage and then adding the former Nissen huts factory, producing furniture in mass production quantities. He then purchased the ailing Lebetkin group (see above) in 1957, and there was phenomenal growth in the 1960's. In 1974 Schreiber Furniture merged with Hotpoint and Morphy Richards, part of the G.E.C. empire, to add kitchen cabinets to their production range, and the final development was an enormous factory and warehouse at Runcorn, Cheshire, which opened in 1979.

My personal connection with Chaim Schreiber goes back to the 1950's when he pioneered the sale to Woolworth's of coffee tables packaged in "knock-down" form. Massil's of Marshmoor cooperated with Schreiber in the innovative production of "contemporary" tapered legs using threaded wooden blocks affixed to the underside of the plywood top, and Schreiber's ordered these in relatively vast quantities culminating in a huge order for 250,000 legs and blocks.

Chaim Schreiber died in May 1984, and the family sold the operating furniture business in 1987, whilst still retaining the property assets including the Runcorn factory.

CHAPTER 9

Immigrant Furniture Makers
in Provincial Towns

My original intention was to limit my researches to London as the majority of immigrants came to the metropolis. However, the situation was replicated in several provincial towns near the ports of entry, and it is worth recording the towns where they settled and giving brief details of a few of the furniture firms that were set up and flourished there.

GLASGOW

H. Morris was formed by Hyman Morris in Glasgow followed by his son Neil, who was succeeded in turn by his son Robert who is now running the business. Hyman Morris was reputed to be one of the outstanding experimenters in the trade, particularly in shaped plywood, and the firm is possibly the only firm of immigrant origin that was involved in the production of furniture for the shipping industry flourishing in Clydeside, including the production of the interiors of liners such as The Queen Mary, and the Queens Elizabeth I and II.

B. Sakol & Sons was run by Jack, Bernard and Malcolm Sakol and is still functioning with members of the next generation.

L. Levin & Sons was set up by Leon Levin whose son, Barnett carried on producing mainly occasional furniture. Apart from being a skilled cabinet maker, Barnett was also an able amateur violinist

Sragovitz & Gillman produced upholstery in Glasgow.

NEWCASTLE

I. Caller & Sons was a company formed by Isaac Caller at the turn of the century. He was joined by his son Louis, who migrated to London to set up as a plywood-merchant in the 1930's, and, later still, established the firm of S.J. Alan in Edmonton to manufacture bedroom suites, the "S" and "J" being named after his daughters, one of whom, June Jacobs, is very active in the Jewish community today.

Axelrod made general cabinet furniture.

Faith Brothers specialized in bedsteads in timber and iron, and also set up a manufacturing branch in Stratford, East London, making wooden bedsteads.

LEEDS

Leeds Cabinet Works, Ladybridge Cabinet Co and **L. Lightman & Sons** were all formed by immigrants and all became part of a conglomerate known as the Ditchburn Group which was run by Mark and Gus Segal. They became professional managers and derived from a furniture background in the East End of London. Three generations of the same Lightman family have become members of the legal profession, one of whom, Gavin, was recently appointed a judge.

Chechik made very ornate reproduction furniture while **I & H Goldberg** made bedroom furniture.

SUNDERLAND

Quite a large number of firms sprang up here. The main companies were as follows:

M. Davies & Sons in which Morris Davies was joined by his three sons, Abraham, Myer and Israel.

Brewer & Co specializing in bedsteads.

Linskill set up and run by Jack Linskill.

Bernstein Brothers, upholsterers.

Mayfair Cabinet Works, run by Sam Finkel who later joined Louis Caller in London as his works manager in the firm of S.J. Alan in Edmonton (*see above*).

LIVERPOOL

The firm of **Rosenblatt** set up in Liverpool specializing in china cabinets.

M & S Shifrin became quite a large producer of dining room suites.

Mersey Bedding Co. made divans.

MANCHESTER

Cyril Bernstein made occasional furniture, and is now one of the largest furniture firms in the North of England producing all types of furniture.

Freedlands specialized in dining room suites and were eventually taken over by Isaac Wolfson's G.U.S. retailing and manufacturing empire.

SHEFFIELD

Sheffield Cabinet Co Ltd was formed by Berel Hyman in the early part of the twentieth century.

BIRMINGHAM

It appears that there were a number of small furniture making firms of immigrant origin in Birmingham at the turn of the century, but none of them was of any consequence or size. Names such as King-Marks, Solomon, Flohm and Levy appear in the records, but **Gordon & Co** stands out as a very substantial firm employing several hundred workers in the early 1900's.

A whole range of furniture was made including bedding and theatre seating. The factory was bombed in the Second World War and the company then ceased to exist.

I am indebted for this information to Zoe Josephs and her book *Birmingham Jewry: More Aspects 1740-1930.*

NORTHAMPTON

The Rest Assured Bedding Company was started by Elias Heymanson (1871-1947), a Jew of Swedish origin who served his apprenticeship to an upholsterer in Birmingham. He set up his own upholstery business in Northampton in 1898. After his death in 1947, his son Dennis carried on the family business of W. D. Heymanson & Co, which he developed into a very large public company known as Rest Assured Bedding Company.

CHAPTER 10

Suppliers of Raw Materials and Components

When they set up in business in England, immigrants had to locate sources of supply for timber, plywood, veneers, cabinet hardware, mirrors etc. There were a considerable number of these firms already in existence in the East End of London, but the indications are that many companies supplying such materials were set up by immigrants to supply other immigrants. They were mainly Jewish in background and the principals had initially been employees in furniture factories. They had thus built up the necessary capital to finance stocks and had acquired the requisite skills in the English language and culture to deal with manufacturers and importers of the materials which they could then sell on.

The furniture makers typically obtained their supplies of materials each week. These were then often delivered on barrows. If the supplier was paid on time at the end of each week, the maker could then go into the timberyard or shop and order his next week's supply. The following is a selection, including both Jewish and older established non-Jewish firms in the area.

TIMBER MERCHANTS

Most makers were producing furniture from solid hardwood at this time, and therefore the timber merchants were the most important suppliers. Hardly any merchants had any kilning facilities and the timber was normally sold sufficiently dried in various ways over time.

The following are some of the many timber yards to be found in many of the streets of East London:

- Hoxton Street boasted **North Eastern Timber Co**. and **L. Lambert**. The latter was run by an eccentric "gentleman of the old school" who could expound on a whole range of diverse subjects from English and Russian literature, politics, philosophy and world economics. I can recall that a group of us in the 1930's would listen to him in wonder over coffee or lunch in the Express Dairy Restaurant in Old Street, whilst he held forth in Russified English on all these subjects and many more;

- **Twitchett**, an old-established merchant in Goldsmith Row, Hackney Road, specialized in Japanese and Austrian Oak;

- **C. Blumson** and **George Holt**, both of Kingsland Road, specialized in Canadian birch which was much used at that time for frames for upholstered furniture;

- **Cripps & Son** of Warner Place, Hackney Road, specialized in American Black Walnut;

- **Baltimore Lumber Co** of Brick Lane dealt in American Red and White Oak;

- **Cobbetts Newling** and **Charik Brothers**, both of Virginia Road, Shoreditch, the former specializing in Japanese and Austrian Oak;

- **J. Matthias** and **L. Matthias** of Hackney Road;

- **James Latham**, a very old-established firm in Curtain Road, selling mouldings as well as unprocessed timber, later became a very large firm in Clapton with branches in provincial towns;

-   **Griew Brothers** of Coronet Street, Old Street, specialists in
    Japanese Oak, related to the older furniture making company
    of I. Griew & Co;

-   **Richenberg** of Great Eastern St;

-   **Tosh & Co** of Hare St, later expanded onto a large site in
    Stamford Hill;

-   **E. Sherry** of Satchwell Rents, Bethnal Green, who later became
    a very large supplier of all types of timber and allied materials;

-   Several firms of the **Goodman** family.

All the above firms would carry large stocks of a whole range of
timbers in addition to the specialities noted above.

PLYWOOD AND VENEERED PANEL MERCHANTS

Plywood could be purchased from **L. Caller** (from Newcastle) in
Old Sreet, and **Elwil Ply** in Rivington Sreet. **James Latham** and
Tosh also became important suppliers of this relatively new
material.

Plywood covered in decorative veneers came from **Austin Veneered
Panel** (later AVP), and **Shadbolt & Sons** in Austin Street, of
Shoreditch and later at Chingford on the North Circular Road.
Another large firm supplying veneered panels, **Berman Brothers,**
started out as cabinet hardware suppliers in Hare Street, Bethnal
Green, and subsequently took large premises in Edmonton, having
absorbed **Times Veneer**.

VENEERS

Veneers were obtainable from:

- **Crispin** of Curtain Road, **Aaronson Bros** of Old Sreet and **W. Isaac Brine** of New North Road;

- **Reliance Veneer Co** of Hackney Road, set up by Mr Lawrence, an immigrant former cabinet maker;

- **Mallinson's**, a very old established timber merchant, who also supplied the highest quality veneers.

CABINET HARDWARE

- **I. Warshaw** of Old Street and **Unerman** of Hackney Road, were large suppliers. Unerman's was originally founded by a cabinet maker at Lebus' factory in Tottenham who sold tools to his co-workers, and whose descendants developed the company into general suppliers.

- **Wilkes Berger** was formed by an alliance between a Mr Wilkes and a Mr Berger, who had been a cabinet maker;

- **S. Greenman** of Pitfield Street and then Old Street, and **H. Greenman** of Hackney Road;

WOODTURNING AND CARVING

Furniture makers normally went to outside suppliers for items such as legs, stretchers, columns, pilasters, pateras, wooden knobs and all turned and twisted items. Specialist woodturning firms in East

London, normally consisting of five or six employees in the earlier part of the 20th century, included:

- **D.Simons** of Hackney Road (*op cit*);
- **B. Jacobsfield** and **Hartz,** both of Rivington Street, EC2;
- **Malin & Leci** of Dunloe Street, Hackney Road;
- **Franklin & Goldberg** of Hackney Road;
- **Withrington Brothers** of Church Street, Bethnal Green, and
- **Massils** (*op cit)* then based in Coronet Street and Hoxton Street, N.1.

The carvers normally worked on their own or with one or two employees at the most, often working on legs produced by the woodturners but also on panels and fascias produced by the cabinet makers themselves. Among the carvers were:

- **Shoolheifer** of Hackney Road, who worked with his sons;
- **M. Berman** and **I. Bronstein**, who produced very high class work for firms such as Beresford & Hicks (*op cit*) and **Sadovsky & Shipman** of Luke Street, Shoreditch.

MACHINERY

Initially, as indicated previously, most of the small workshops made furniture by hand. However, slowly, as firms grew and the owners wished to mechanise, they started purchasing simple plant - circular saws, bandsaws, spindles, mortising machines and the like. This plant was mainly second-hand and had been reconditioned, particularly by two (non-immigrant) firms - Wilkinsons of Bethnal Green and Cooksley of Tabernacle Street, near Curtain Road. Only later would the firms have resources to purchase new plant from foreign makers with East End showrooms like Danckaert, Guilliet, Interwood and Schubert, and from indigenous engineering manufacturers, Wadkin and Brookman of Leicester and Cubbage of High Wycombe.

GENERAL

The Warshaw family became general providers in the trade; among their companies were **North Eastern Timber** supplying timber and plywood, **I. Warshaw** supplying cabinet hardware and **Clarke & Co.** of Drysdale Street, Shoreditch, for mirrors and plate glass.

CHAPTER 11

CONCLUSIONS

There is no doubt that the immigrant furniture workers who arrived in the latter part of the 19th century and early 20th century made a significant contribution to the development of the British furniture industry during the 20th century. As already mentioned, the second and third generations of descendants of these immigrants have now tended to enter the professions, commerce and the arts, and indeed all my four children have followed this path.

Among all the immigrants I have mentioned, however, I feel I should single out four in particular, who were, in my view, outstanding in the development of the British furniture industry in the 20th century. These individuals had either been born overseas themselves or were the children of immigrants. They are Harris Lebus, Luciano Ercolani, Ray Hille and Chaim Schreiber.

Harris Lebus (1852-1907)
When Harris Lebus took over the running of the business on the death of his father in 1879, as the older son, he inherited a small firm spread over a few workshops in the East End. By 1903 he had built an extraordinarily large factory on a 13.5 acre site at Tottenham which was at that time on the very edge of London. This would have been fully equipped with the most up-to-date machinery at the time but employed over 1,000 factory workers. Only four years later, by the time of his death at the age of 55, *The Cabinet Maker* in its obituary (see Appendix 3) said that Lebus had become one of the largest furniture factories in the world, employing between 3,000 and 4,000 workers. All this had been achieved in about 25 years.

Ray Hille (1901-1986)

Like Lebus, but fifty years later, Ray Hille joined a firm already established earlier by her immigrant father, having had some training as a designer. On his retirement, she took over the running of the firm which was then devoted to the production of ornate period-style furniture of the highest quality, together with a few items in modern styles which she had designed. After struggling on through the war years, she rebuilt the firm with her daughter and son-in-law, but her most important contribution was the encouragement of Robin Day in 1949 and her total commitment to producing only modern designs henceforth, using up-to-date materials and techniques including shaped plywood, metal, plastics and glass which had developed in wartime aircraft production. There is no doubt that under her direction Hille's became outstanding both nationally and internationally in the modern furniture field.

Luciano Ercolani (1885-1975)

In my opinion Ercolani's contribution to the trade was his unprecedented use of English Elm combined with beech turnings in a unique range of furniture which he developed from a traditional English style of country furniture. Like Ray Hille he had been producing conventional furniture before the War but, only after the end of the Utility furniture regime, was he inspired to produce in large quantities furniture combining a particular English Arts and Crafts style with the beauty and sometimes wild grain of an economic timber never previously used for cabinet furniture. The Ercol company, still in family hands, remains very active and successful, making characteristic use of hardwoods such as oak and ash together with beech and elm in an extended range of domestic and contract furniture.

Chaim Schreiber (1918-1984).

Here is an example of a young man, an engineer and would-be architect with an artistic talent for marquetry, who came to this country from Europe in 1938. Little did he know that he was escaping the Holocaust that was to come, but his career was characterized by the intelligence, training and vision he brought to the industry, and from 1944 he was able to build up in a short period one of the largest and most successful furniture companies in the furniture industry.

He asked me once with a smile: "Do you know why I can beat all those furniture people ?" "Why?" I responded. "Because I am not a cabinet maker !" In fact he very much planned his development and produced furniture using engineering rather than craft principles and showed consummate skill and judgement in delegating functions and responsibilities to his staff. This is of course in stark contrast to the normal picture of many furniture making companies that I knew which, typically, were run by the descendants of cabinet makers who tried to do everything themselves.

In some ways these four exceptional people were also typical of the many immigrant families who arrived between 1881 and 1939 - mostly Jewish - who eventually set up a large number of furniture making firms, mainly in and around the East End of London.

It took most of them ten to twenty years to set up their own firm (although there seem to have been several who set up on their own very soon after their arrival). Particularly for immigrants, the intervening period of World War I must have been extremely difficult due to shortage of materials, lack of a retail market and large element of xenophobia. However, many survived, were through the years of the Depression (1929-31) and built up very substantial companies which became involved in various forms of war work between 1939 and 1945.

Many flourished in the post-war boom, mainly producing versions of the same sorts of furniture which they had made in the 1930's with the exceptions mentioned. In my view, by this time, these firms of immigrant origin accounted for about half of the employees in the London furniture industry. Of the firms founded by immigrants still functioning today, however, very few are still run on a family basis.

In fact, the whole British furniture industry, in common with many others, has been decimated over the last two or three decades. A large proportion - as much as fifty percent - of furniture in the High Street shops in Britain today is of foreign manufacture and much is based on reproductions of traditional English and other styles, but imported from countries as diverse as Taiwan, USA, Italy, Spain and many others.

Yet I see a glimmer of hope for the British furniture industry in the generations of craftsmen and craftswomen emerging, whose emphasis is on the design and production of fine furniture, usually custom-made in small workshops.

The sources of this movement derive from:

) **Edward Barnsley Workshops** at Froxfield, near Petersfield in Hampshire, established in the 1920's and now functioning as an educational trust. Here, paid apprentices are trained in the indigenous Barnsley/Gimson/William Morris tradition which we have already mentioned elsewhere.

b) **John Makepeace and his Parnham College** in Dorset, established in 1977, from which about a dozen craftspeople - men and women - have graduated each year after a generally self-financed two-year intensive course of furniture-designing and -making, management techniques, costing and administration.

c) In addition to the many state-run **art colleges and technical colleges**, where the emphasis is on good modern design which the students make to the highest standards of craftsmanship, many of the graduates of these establishments then set up their own independent **workshops** to produce furniture and woodwork to commission by private individuals and institutions.

d) **Comprehensive exhibitions** of the work of individual furniture-makers who have graduated from these establishments. These shows both generate sales of the pieces exhibited and lead to commissions for new works, and are typified by the exhibitions organized and promoted on a regular basis by Betty Norbury in Cheltenham.

e) Another hopeful sign is that the **Geffrye Museum** in East London (where most immigrants first established themselves) has an important development scheme being built with the assistance of National Lottery funding. Part of this development is planned to house an exhibition of fine modern furniture designed and produced by the graduates of the various establishments mentioned above. In my view, British mass manufacturers will benefit from this innovation, as the more enterprising among themcould adapt some of these designs on a commercial scale in their own factories

At the same time such a permanent, but changing, public display may also enhance the appreciation of contemporary design among the British public generally. After all, if Chippendale, Hepplewhite and Sheraton had persisted in reproducing previous styles such as

Tudor, Jacobean, William and Mary and Queen Anne, we would have been denied the wonderful "modern" pieces that these designers themselves evolved in the eighteenth century, which now form part of our national heritage.

REFERENCES

Frank Austin: *Speech at Opening of Exhibition at the Geffrye Museum,* Jewish Historical Society of England (London, 1987) (on tape)

J.C. Baum & M. Glick: *Heritage No 1- An Historical Series on the Jewish Inhabitants of North London* (London,1982)

Harry Blacker: *Just like it was - Memoirs of the Mittel East* (London, 1974)

Charles Booth: *The Life and Labour of the People in London* (London, 1888)

B. Cohen & Sons Ltd: *A Century of Progress in the Furniture Industry* (London, 1947)

Luciano Ercolani: *A Furniture Maker* (Tonbridge, 1975)

Sorrel Hershberg: Elegance and Comfort: HK Chairs and Settees, in *Things* (London, Summer 1997)

Kenneth Hudson: *Where We Used to Work* (London, 1980)

Zoe Josephs: *Birmingham Jewry - More Aspects 1740-1930 (Birmingham, 1984)*

Pat Kirkham, Rodney Mace, Julia Porter: *Furnishing the World. the East End Furniture Trade 1830-1980* (London, 1987)

Louis S. Lebus: *History of Harris Lebus - 1840 to 1947* (private publication)

Vivian D.Lipman: *A Social History of the Jews in England 1850-1950* (London, 1954)

Sutherland Lyall: *Hille - 75 Years of British Furniture* (London, 1981)

Henry Mayhew: 'Of the Furniture Workers', Letter LXIII *Morning Chronicle* 1 August, 1850

Henry Mayhew: 'Of the Fancy Cabinet Makers', Letter LXIV *Morning Chronicle* 8 August, 1850

Henry Mayhew: 'Of the Garret Masters', Letter LXV *Morning Chronicle* 22 August, 1850

Ewart Myer: *Myer's First Century 1876-1967* (London, 1976)

Hew Reid: *The Furniture Makers - A History of Trade Unionism in the Furniture trade 1868-1972* (Oxford, 1986)

Sir George Trevelyan: *Tribute from a Pupil* (Gimson Exhibition, Leicester Museum & Art Gallery, 1969)

Anthony Vaughan: The Vaughans: *East End Furniture Makers - A History of Trade Unionism in the Furniture Trade 1868-1972* (Oxford, 1968)

Appendix 1

DATE OF UK ARRIVAL	NAME OF IMMIGRANT:	DATE OF BIRTH:	ORIGINATING FROM:
	APPENDIX 1: CHRONOLOGICAL LIST OF SOME IMMIGRANT FURNITURE WORKERS IN THE U.		
1815	Abraham MYER	1796	Rhineland, GERMANY
1840	Lewis LEBUS	1817	Breslau, GERMANY
?	Barnett COHEN	1815	?
1867	Morris RUBEN	1864	Vilna, LITHUANIA
1870	Julius B BERESFORD (was WISZNIEWSKI)	?	POLAND
1873	Domenico BIANCO	1852	Piedmont, ITALY
1874	Philip David BURKLE (was BUERKLE)	1844	Schmiden, SOUTH GERMANY
1874	Jacob ZINKIN	?	RUSSIA
1884	? POSTER	?	?
1884	Morris COHEN	1872	Antopol, RUSSIA
1885	Simon SADOVSKY	1865	RUSSIA
1887	Isaac Jacob SKLANOWITZ	1864	Kolno, EAST POLAND
1890	Isaac GRIEW	1870	Vilna, LITHUANIA
1890	Morris EPSTEIN	?	RUSSIA
1890	Isaac WISEMAN	1875	Czernowitz, RUMANIA
1891	Davis SIMONS	1874	Warsaw, POLAND
1891	Barnet ABRAHAMS	1890	Plotsk, RUSSIA
1893	Harry YAGER	1879	RUMANIA
1894	NATHAN BLOOM	1880	Bialystok, POLAND
1895	? CARAS	?	?
1895	Nathan STEINBERG	1880	Tarnopol, AUSTRIA
1896	Jack CINNAMON	1887	POLAND
1898	Mark GINSBERG	1875	?
1898	Marcus ORNSTEIN	1870	AUSTRIA
1898	Jack LUBELSKY	1873	Grodno, RUSSIA
1898	Maurice EDOLOFF	1876	Vitebsk, RUSSIA
1898	? BROOKES (was BROOKENTHAL)	?	?
1898	? FRANKLIN	1874	RUMANIA
1898	Bernard GABE	1879	Odessa, UKRAINE
1898	Luciano ERCOLANI	1885	Tuscany, ITALY
1899	Peter WAALS (was VAN DER WAALS)	1870	The Hague, HOLLAND
1900	Nathan AGRAN	1877	Chrernigov, UKRAINE
1900	Hyman BERMAN	1880	Pinsk, RUSSIA
1900	Salomon HILLE	1875	UKRAINE
1900	Barnett VIDELSKY	?	Kovno LITHUANIA
1903	Solomon ARENSON	1879	Ula, Vitebsk, RUSSIA
1903	Barnett ROSENBERG	1873	UKRAINE
1904	Julius TAYLOR (was SCHNEIDER)	1879	UKRAINE
1905	Hyman MASSIL	1881	Azarich,BYELORUSSIA
1905	Barnett SEROTA	1880	Zhitomir, RUSSIA
1905	Harris LEBETKIN	1884	Grodno, RUSSIA
1905	Reuben BLUESTONE	1890	LITHUANIA
1905	Reuben SERLIN	1885	Yalowka, POLAND
1906	Mark DOCTORS	1876	Odessa, UKRAINE
1906	Lazarus SERLIN	?	Yalowka, POLAND
1907	Simon WEINTROB	1887	AUSTRIA
1908	Jack SANDERS (was SENDEROVITCH)	1892	Azarich,BYELORUSSIA
1908	Joseph SERLIN	?	Yalowka, POLAND
1910	George SERLIN (was Gershon SERLIN)	?	Yalowka, POLAND
1911	Lazarus FINEMAN	1891	?
1911	Israel BURKE (was BERCOVICI)	1884	RUMANIA
1912	Isaac NATHAN	1891	Minsk, RUSSIA
1912	Barnett NATHAN	1896	Minsk, RUSSIA
1912	Norman NATHAN	1905	Minsk, RUSSIA
1912	Joseph RURKA	1891	Kiev, UKRAINE
1912	Gershon STAMP	1881	Kiev, UKRAINE
1914	? APPLEBAUM	?	UKRAINE
?	? LEWIS (was LAZEMNIKOFF)	?	?
1914	Baruch NEWMAN (Was NEUMANN)	1874	Rozwadow, POLAND
1923	Samuel ENGLENDER	1902	Warsaw, POLAND
1933	Howard KEITH (was Hans KREBS)	1902	Berlin, GERMANY
1938	Chaim S. SCHREIBER	1918	Lwow, POLAND

ARTS U.K. BINESS IN:	COMMERCIAL ACTIVITY IN U.K.
1876	Son, Horatio, purchases iron bedstead firm in Vauxhall, London, & forms Horatio Myer & Co.
1857	L. Lebus (Whitechapel) > Harris Lebus(mass production furniture manufacturers)
1848	B.Cohen > B.Cohen & Sons (very high quality furniture of all sorts)
1887	Morris Ruben
1891	Forms Beresford & Hicks with royal warrant (very high quality domestic/boardroom furniture)
1880	D.Bianco & Sons (Bespoke domestic & boardroom furniture)
1881	D. Burkle & Sons (high quality domestic, later boardroom furniture and joinery)
?	Zinkin & Sons
1900	Stickmaker & woodturner
1896	Cabinetmakers>veneer merchants>laminate manufacturers as Bonded Laminates Ltd
1896	S.Sadovsky > Beautility Furniture (domestic furniture)
1889	Sklan
1895	Woodcarver > I. Griew & Co
1913	Starts in Gun St, E1, sons form H&L Epstein making reproduction furniture in Hanbury St
?	Starts in East End > Ducal Furniture, later pioneering mass production of pine furniture in Andover
1922	Woodturner> D & J Simons
1920	Mitchell & Barnet (china cabinets and bookcases)
1900	London Plywood & Timber Co (merchants)+ Moss & Partners (desking)
1900	N. Bloom (made high grade bedroom suites). Ceases in 1935
1902	Works for Lebus, then forms Stern & Caras with brother-in-law
1910	> Stonehill Furniture (general domestic furniture)
1914	J.Cinnamon>Cintique Furniture (showwood upholstery)
1910	Ginsberg. Ceases in 1914.
1902	Settles in Plymouth, making bamboo furniture>son, Frank > F.Austin > Austinsuite (London)
1898	J. Lubesky & Sons>Lucas Furniture Systems (office furniture)
1900	Edoloff & Sons
?	Brookenthal Brothers (bedroom suites)
1900	Woodturners>Franklin & Goldberg
?	Woodcarver forms Gabe & Pass with brother-in-law Pass
1920	Works for Fredk Parker and Gomme in High Wycombe > pioneers new technology as Ercol Furniture
1920	Chief cabinetmaker for Ernest Gimson at Sapperton>own firm (one-off, highest quality pieces)
1901	Nathan Agran(mid-quality domestic furniture)
1916	Ironmongers > Berman Brothers. (veneered plywood)
1906	S. Hille > S. Hille & Co (high quality, up to WWII reproduction, then modern contract/office furniture
1906	B. Dell & Son
1919	Starts to make oak domestic furniture>Arenson Group (office furniture)
?	Worked at S. Hille
1919	Messrs. Taylor
1912	Woodturner, forms H & M Massil > Massils of Marshmoor
1911	Serota & Cohen
1917	Messrs Lebetkin
1919	Worked for Elevitsky>Bluestone & Elvin
1910	Later forms Validity Furniture
1907	Makes china cabinets in Bacon St, E.2. with 2 brothers
1910	Later forms L. Serlin & Sons
1916	Winthrop Brothers (dining room furniture)
1921	J.Sanders in Rivington St, E.C.2.
1910	Later forms J. Serlin & Sons
1910	Later forms G. Serlin & Sons
?	Son, Sydney, becomes secretary of furniture Trade Union
1917	Berkovitch>Olympus Furniture
1916	}
1916	}Form B & I Nathan (cabinet furniture manufacturers)
1916	}
1921	Rurka & Son (bedstead-makers)
1921	Stamp & Son
?	Applebaum & Son
?	Forms Kings Cabinet Co
1919	Plywood/veneering > Alan Newman>Newman Group (contract joinery & furniture)
1926	Upholsterer in London, then moved from East End to Weybridge to Derbyshire in contracts market.
1933	H.K. Furniture , very high quality upholstery of modern design; later also cabinet manufacturing
1944	Lordship Products>Schreiber Wood Industries (general cabinet & kitchen furniture)

Appendix 2

Furniture Workshops in the East End, early 1920's

Reproduced from *Where We Used to Work* by Kenneth Hudson, published by John Baker, London, 1980.

The figure against each street represents the total number of workshops and the figure in brackets the number with obviously Jewish names.

Allenby Road	1 (1)
Amberley Street	1 (1)
Arline Street	1 (0)
Arnos Road	1 (0)
Assembly Passage	1 (1)
Audrey Street	1 (0)
Austin Street	10 (9)
Bacon Street	4 (4)
Bedford Street	1 (1)
Ben Jonson Road	2 (1)
Bethnal Green Road	18 (9)
Bishops Road	2 (0)
Bishop's Row	1 (0)
Bonner Street	1 (0)
Boundary Street	7 (2)
Brick Lane	29 (23)
Brook Street	1 (0)
Broomsbury Street	1 (1)
Brown Yard, Temple Street	1 (0)
Brunswick Street	4 (3)
Buckhurst Street	1 (1)
Busby Street	2 (2)
Buxton Street	8 (7)
Cable Street	2 (2)
Calvert Avenue	2 (2)
Cambridge Road	1 (1)
Chambord Street	2 (2)
Charles Street	1 (1)
Cheshire Street	1 (1)
Chicksand Street	1 (1)
Chiltern Street	2 (1)
Christian Street	3 (3)
Church Court	1 (1)
Church Row	2 (1)
Church Street	11 (11)
Club Row	5 (3)
Coate Street	1 (1)
Coke Street	1 (1)
Columbia Market	3 (2)
Columbia Road	28 (19)
Columbia Street	1 (1)
Commercial Road	4 (3)
Commercial Street	1 (1)
Cosser Street	1 (0)
Cremer Street	1 (1)
Cutler Street	1 (1)
Cygnet Street	1 (1)
Dock Street	1 (0)
Dunloe Street	5 (3)
Ebor Street	1 (3)

Elder Street	1 (1)	Hassard Street	3 (2)
Exmouth Street	1 (1)	Henna Street	2 (2)
Ezra Street	4 (2)	Hocker Street	12 (11)
		Hollybush Gardens	1 (0)
Finch Street	1 (1)	Houndsditch Road	1 (0)
Florida Street	1 (0)	Hows Street	2 (1)
Fountain Street	2 (2)	Hulton Street	1 (1)
Fournier Street	1 (1)		
Francis Street	1 (0)	Joan Street	1 (1)
French Place, Shoreditch	1 (0)	Jubilee Street	1 (1)
Fuller Road	1 (1)		
Fuller Street	1 (1)	Kay Street	1 (1)
		Kerbela Street	2 (2)
Gayneland Road	1 (0)	Kingsland Road	26 (17)
Gibraltrar Walk	22 (13)	Laburnum Grove	1 (1)
Globe Road	8 (5)	Laburnum Street	1 (1)
Goldsmith's Row	10 (3)	Lark Row	1 (1)
Gossett Street	5 (2)	Little Peare Street	1 (1)
Granby Street	1 (1)		
Great Cambridge Street	3 (2)	Mansfield Street	1 (0)
Great Eagle Street	1 (1)	Mansford Road	2 (1)
Great Peare Street	6(6)	Mansford Street	1 (0)
Great Pell Street	2 (2)	Mansworth Court	1 (1)
Green Street	3 (2)	Margaret Place	1 (0)
Greenfield Court	1 (1)	Marlin Road	1 (0)
Greenfield Street	1 (1)	Mile End Road	7 (3)
Grimsby Street	1 (1)	Mount Street	6 (5)
Gun Street	2 (2)		
		Newlyn Street	1 (1)
Hackney Road	37 (20)		
Half Moon Passage	1 (1)	Oatley Road	1 (1)
Hanbury Street	4 (4)	Old Bethnal Green Road	1 (0)
Hare Street	19 (16)	Old Ford Road	1 (0)

Old Ford Street	2 (0)	Sidney Street	1 (1)
Old Montague Street	2 (2)	Spital Street	1 (1)
Old Nichol Street	1 (0)	Stamford Place	1 (0)
Osborne Street	1 (1)		
Oxford Street	1 (1)	Teesdale Street	11 (5)
		Temple Street	9 (3)
Pearson Street	2 (0)	Tuilerie Street	3 (0)
Pedley Street	2 (2)	Turin Street	2 (1)
Pelham Street	2 (2)		
Peter Street	2 (2)	Umberston Street	1 (1)
Plumber's Row	1 (1)		
Pollard Row	1 (0)	Vallance Road	3 (3)
Prince's Court	4 (4)	Vandon Street	1 (1)
Printbury, Print Place	1 (1)	Virginia Road	16 (14)
Pritchard's Road	1 (0)		
		Waltham Place	1 (0)
Rapley Place	2 (1)	Watney Street	1 (1)
Ravenscroft Street	7 (4)	Wentworth Street	1 (1)
Ravenshill Street	1 (0)	Weymouth Terrace	5 (2)
Roan Horse Yard	5 (1)	Whitechapel Road	2 (2)
Robert Court	1 (0)	Willow Court	1 (0)
Robinson Road	1 (0)	Winchester Street	3 (2)
Rupert Place	1 (1)		

St. George's Street 1 (1)
St. Peter's Street 1 (0)
Sale Street 1 (1)
Satchwell Street 1 (0)
Sclater Street 5 (5)
Sewardstone Road 1 (0)
Sheffie Place 1 (1)
Shepherd Street 1 (1)
Shoreditch High Street 2 (1)

DEATH OF MR. HARRIS LEBUS.

A REMARKABLE CAREER.

FEW men in the furniture trade have had such a career as Mr. Harris Lebus. We remember the beginnings of it nearly 40 years ago, and as we look back over the struggles and successes of this remarkable business man we cannot refrain from adding our testimony to the qualities and character which enabled him to triumph over all his difficulties. If ever a cabinet maker started at the bottom rung of the ladder, Mr. Lebus did. We seem to see him now bringing the work of the week from his little workshop in Wellclose Square for the inspection of some of the Curtain Road factors. There was something in the keen eye, the determined step and the never-failing vivacity of the compact little man that betokened exceptional qualities. Nothing could damp his optimism or destroy his ardour. And so, from step to step, from the making of the humblest kind of " Duchesse Table and Stand," he climbed upwards and founded one of the largest and best-managed furniture factories in the country, if not in the world. He was among the first to " think imperially " in cabinet making. He bought his timber by the shipload and ransacked the machine shops of the world for the most up-to-date appliances. He was the first to press the wonderful carving machine into the service of woodworking, and no new invention of whatever class escaped his observant and practical eye.

Some critic, in speaking of Lord Beaconsfield, said of him, " To become what he is from what he was is the greatest wonder of all." This may be truly said of Mr. Lebus. We know of no more remarkable instance of perseverance and industry. He did not know the word " can't." It was always " we will," and he did. Over and above his business activities he had a kind heart for the charities and amenities of life. His good work in connection with the F.B.A. will always be remembered with gratitude. He was a good father, a loyal friend, and one of the men of our times whose career stands out even among the most remarkable instances of success in the history of our trade.

* * *

Mr. Harris Lebus was born in Hull fifty-five years ago, and had been engaged in the furniture industry for thirty-five years. His first workshops and factories were at Wellclose Square, but twenty-four years ago he opened showrooms in Tabernacle Street, on the site of his present extensive premises. Five years ago the factory was transferred from London to Tottenham, and is one of the largest furniture factories in the world, the total number of employees being between three and four thousand.

The illness which terminated fatally on Saturday was of long standing. The funeral took place at Willesden Cemetery on Sunday, and there were present a large number of friends and relatives and the heads of all the departments of the factory and business.

Mr. Lebus was treasurer of the Furniture Trades' Benevolent and Provident Association, and the Association, which sent a wreath, was represented by Mr. F. W. Avant (chairman), Mr. Charles Dunk (hon. secretary), and Mr. W. D. Newton (secretary).

The Late Mr. Harris Lebus.

Obituary of Harris Lebus from *The Cabinet Maker*, September 1907. *By permission of The British Library.*

OBITUARY.

Mr. HARRIS LEBUS.

We regret to report the death of Mr. Harris Lebus which occurred at 11, Netherhall Gardens, Hampstead, on Saturday morning. Mr. Lebus had

Mr. Harris Lebus.

been in failing health for a long time past and had not been expected to live through the preceding week, but he had rallied somewhat and the end came rather unexpectedly.

Mr. Lebus was a remarkable personality both in the Jewish community and in the country. His career was an extraordinary record of the rise of a man from small beginnings to a position of enormous commercial influence. It was one of the fairy tales of commerce. The present writer, who knew him intimately, can say without hesitation that he owed his success and position to nothing but his own force of character, his indomitable energy and perseverance, his giant mind and the wise counsel and devoted attachment of his wife. He was born in Hull 55 years ago and came to London as a child. He was educated at the Jews' Free School of which, in later years, he was a liberal supporter and he always was pleased and proud to maintain his friendship with his old teacher, Mr. Myer Davis, for whom he entertained great affection. He left school quite a boy and commenced to work at the bench. He was determined to get on and did not mind how hard he worked, and he has often told me how he economised his few pence and wheeled, for miles, a barrow with the materials for his work. He was quite a youth when he set up in business for himself as a maker of furniture and by small stages of advancement, at first, and then by leaps and bounds, he built up what is probably the greatest cabinet manufactory in the world. Some few years ago, he turned his enormous factories in Tabernacle Street into show-rooms and built at Tottenham the great factories which constitute quite a town in themselves and gave employment to thousands. His great intellect grasped every detail of his mighty business and it can be said of him, with perfect truth, that he was the soul of honour and straightforwardness and there was no taint upon one shilling of his great fortune.

Mr. Lebus was quite unspoiled by success. His head never grew dizzy and his heart never grew selfish. He gave away abundantly and never refused his assistance and the kindly and wise advice that was even more valuable at times than the pecuniary help with which he was so ready. He hated fuss and publicity concerning his charities. His personal tastes were of the simplest. He was a great reader of character and reckoned up with unerring precision all with whom he came into contact. To be admitted to his friendship meant at least, the cachet of sincerity.

In his own home he was a veritable king. He was idolised by his wife and children and a better husband and father and friend or a happier man it would have been impossible to find. He was proud of being an English Jew. He loved his country and his own people and thought them both the best in the world. He was originally a member of the Great Synagogue. When he moved to Hampstead some 13 years ago, he joined the local synagogue and was for a brief period a member of the Board of Management and counselled the extension of the building (which eventually took place) on a much larger scale than was ultimately adopted. On questions of Jewish observance he was an advanced thinker, but he was loyal to his faith in his heart of hearts and often used to say that where there is no real religion there is no blessing. A week ago, when he felt that his end was approaching, he called his children together and clearly and earnestly exhorted them to remain faithful to his example and teaching. So perfect was the understanding between himself and his family that those interested in the communal charities may feel assured that there will remain the influence of a truly good man whose death in the fulness of his powers and in the prime of his life is a distinct and far-reaching loss. A. A. G.

Obituary of Harris Lebus from *The Jewish Chronicle*, September 1907. *By permission of The British Library.*

Archy Arenson

THE FOUNDER and chairman of office furniture business Arenson, Archy Arenson, has died. He was 67.

Responsible for starting a company which today boasts a staff of 500 and turnover of £38m, Mr Arenson came from humble beginnings.

Born in London to a poor family he was the youngest of seven children, and was orphaned at 13.

He began Arenson from a lock-up garage in north London in 1948, designing the first dinette and kitchenette suites, selling them to John Lewis.

The company suffered a massive fire in 1960, and Mr Arenson had to build up the business again practically from scratch.

Soon after, the night before the opening of the 1964 Earls Court furniture show he decided to concentrate on what was to become President Office Furniture with the Lincoln and Columbus ranges.

It was Mr Arenson who launched the first KD office furniture in the UK.

After moving the company to St Albans, and a 240,000sq ft Hertfordshire factory, Mr Arenson decided to "go public" with the business in 1970.

He passed the executive chairmanship to new owners, Skandinavisk Holding of Copenhagen, in 1988. He remained on the board as non-executive director, and celebrated the company's 40 years at a party held for him last year.

He leaves a wife, Vicki, and three children.

Obituary of Archy Arenson from *The Cabinet Maker*, 12 November 1993. *By permission of The British Library.*

THE JEWISH MUSEUM
London's Museum of Jewish Life

The Jewish Museum opens a window onto the history and religious life of the Jewish community in Britain and beyond. It seeks to recover and preserve the diverse roots and heritage of Jewish people in Britain, and to increase knowledge and understanding about Jewish life and history.

The Jewish Museum, Finchley

Social history displays tracing Jewish immigration and settlement in London. The Museum's exhibition *The Tailor, the Baker, The Cabinet maker ...* looks at Jewish working life in the East End, with reconstructions of cabinet making and tailoring workshops. Holocaust education is also a major feature of the Museum's work and our displays include a moving exhibition on London-born Holocaust survivor, Leon Greenman.

80 East End Road
London N3 2SY
Tel. 0181 349 1143

The Jewish Museum, Camden Town

Attractive galleries illustrating Jewish history and religious life in Britain. The Museum has been awarded Designated status by the Museums and Galleries Commission for its outstanding collections of Jewish ceremonial art, which are among the finest in the world. Audio-visual programmes and changing exhibitions.

Raymond Burton House
129-131 Albert Street
London NW1 7NB
Tel. 0171 284 1997

THE GEFFRYE MUSEUM

The Geffrye Museum is set in 18th century almshouses with attractive gardens in Shoreditch, East London. It is the only museum in the U.K. to specialise in the history of English domestic interiors, displaying English furniture and decorative arts in a series of period rooms from 1600 to the 1950's. It has a related collection of decorative art, paintings, personalia and archives. An extension, planned for 1998, will provide space for galleries on 20th century furniture and interiors.

Kingsland Road
London E2 8EA
Tel. 0171 739 9893